*Photo by Man Ray*

ANTONIN ARTAUD

ANTONIN ARTAUD

*Photo Pastier*

ANTONIN ARTAUD

# THE THEATER AND ITS DOUBLE

# The Theater
## and Its Double

By Antonin Artaud

Translated from the French
by Mary Caroline Richards

**GROVE PRESS**
**NEW YORK**

*Published simultaneously in Canada*
*Printed in the United States of America*

Library of Congress Catalog Card Number 58-9910

ISBN 978-0-8021-5030-1

Grove Press
an imprint of Grove Atlantic
154 West 14th Street
New York, NY 10011

Distributed by Publishers Group West

groveatlantic.com

17 18 19 20     51 50 49 48

# CONTENTS

5

## A NOTE ON THE TRANSLATION

This translation faithfully follows the text of the *Le Théâtre et son Double*, published by Gallimard in *Collection Métamorphoses* as No. IV, copyright 1938.

*"Esprit,"* for which we have no English equivalent, combining as it does both *mind* and *spirit*, has in most cases been translated as "mind." And the expression *"mise en scène"* has been retained throughout, for Artaud's use of it implies all that we call direction, production, and staging.

## PREFACE: The Theater and Culture

Never before, when it is life itself that is in question, has there been so much talk of civilization and culture. And there is a curious parallel between this generalized collapse of life at the root of our present demoralization and our concern for a culture which has never been coincident with life, which in fact has been devised to tyrannize over life.

Before speaking further about culture, I must remark that the world is hungry and not concerned with culture, and that the attempt to orient toward culture thoughts turned only toward hunger is a purely artificial expedient.

What is most important, it seems to me, is not so much to defend a culture whose existence has never kept a man from going hungry, as to extract, from what is called culture, ideas whose compelling force is identical with that of hunger.

We need to live first of all; to believe in what makes us live and that something *makes* us live—to believe that whatever is produced from the mysterious depths of ourselves need not forever haunt us as an exclusively digestive concern.

I mean that if it is important for us to eat first of all, it is even more important for us not to waste in the sole concern for eating our simple power of being hungry.

If confusion is the sign of the times, I see at the root of this confusion a rupture between things and words, between things and the ideas and signs that are their representation.

Not, of course, for lack of philosophical systems; their number and contradictions characterize our old French and

European culture: but where can it be shown that life, our life, has ever been affected by these systems? I will not say that philosophical systems must be applied directly and immediately: but of the following alternatives, one must be true:

Either these systems are within us and permeate our being to the point of supporting life itself (and if this is the case, what use are books?), or they do *not* permeate us and therefore do not have the capacity to support life (and in this case what does their disappearance matter?).

We must insist upon the idea of culture-in-action, of culture growing within us like a new organ, a sort of second breath; and on civilization as an applied culture controlling even our subtlest actions, a *presence of mind*; the distinction between culture and civilization is an artificial one, providing two words to signify an identical function.

A civilized man judges and is judged according to his behavior, but even the term "civilized" leads to confusion: a cultivated "civilized" man is regarded as a person instructed in systems, a person who thinks in forms, signs, representations—a monster whose faculty of deriving thoughts from acts, instead of identifying acts with thoughts, is developed to an absurdity.

If our life lacks brimstone, i.e., a constant magic, it is because we choose to observe our acts and lose ourselves in considerations of their imagined form instead of being impelled by their force.

And this faculty is an exclusively human one. I would even say that it is this infection of the human which contaminates ideas that should have remained divine; for far from believing that man invented the supernatural and the divine, I think it is man's age-old intervention which has ultimately corrupted the divine within him.

All our ideas about life must be revised in a period when nothing any longer adheres to life; it is this painful cleavage which is responsible for the revenge of *things*; the poetry which is no longer within us and which we no longer succeed in finding in things suddenly appears on their wrong side: consider the unprecedented number of crimes whose perverse gratuitousness is explained only by our powerlessness to take complete possession of life.

If the theater has been created as an outlet for our repressions, the agonized poetry expressed in its bizarre corruptions of the facts of life demonstrates that life's intensity is still intact and asks only to be better directed.

But no matter how loudly we clamor for magic in our lives, we are really afraid of pursuing an existence entirely under its influence and sign.

Hence our confirmed lack of culture is astonished by certain grandiose anomalies; for example, on an island without any contact with modern civilization, the mere passage of a ship carrying only healthy passengers may provoke the sudden outbreak of diseases unknown on that island but a specialty of nations like our own: shingles, influenza, grippe, rheumatism, sinusitis, polyneuritis, etc.

Similarly, if we think Negroes smell bad, we are ignorant of the fact that anywhere but in Europe it is we whites who "smell bad." And I would even say that we give off an odor as white as the gathering of pus in an infected wound.

As iron can be heated until it turns white, so it can be said that everything excessive is white; for Asiatics white has become the mark of extreme decomposition.

This said, we can begin to form an idea of culture, an idea which is first of all a protest.

A protest against the senseless constraint imposed upon the idea of culture by reducing it to a sort of inconceivable Pantheon, producing an idolatry no different from the image-worship of those religions which relegate their gods to Pantheons.

A protest against the idea of culture as distinct from life—as if there were culture on one side and life on the other, as if true culture were not a refined means of understanding and *exercising* life.

The library at Alexandria can be burnt down. There are forces above and beyond papyrus: we may temporarily be deprived of our ability to discover these forces, but their energy will not be suppressed. It is good that our excessive facilities are no longer available, that forms fall into oblivion: a culture without space or time, restrained only by the capacity of our own nerves, will reappear with all the more energy. It is right that from time to time cataclysms occur which compel us to return to nature, i.e., to rediscover life. The old totemism of animals, stones, objects capable of discharging thunderbolts, costumes impregnated with bestial essences—everything, in short, that might determine, disclose, and direct the secret forces of the universe—is for us a dead thing, from which we derive nothing but static and aesthetic profit, the profit of an audience, not of an actor.

Yet totemism is an actor, for it moves, and has been created in behalf of actors; all true culture relies upon the barbaric and primitive means of totemism whose savage, i.e., entirely spontaneous, life I wish to worship.

What has lost us culture is our Occidental idea of art and the profits we seek to derive from it. Art and culture cannot be considered together, contrary to the treatment universally accorded them!

True culture operates by exaltation and force, while the European ideal of art attempts to cast the mind into an attitude distinct from force but addicted to exaltation. It is a lazy, unserviceable notion which engenders an imminent death. If the Serpent Quetzalcoatl's multiple twists and turns are harmonious, it is because they express the equilibrium and fluctuations of a sleeping force; the intensity of the forms is there only to seduce and direct a force which, in music, would produce an insupportable range of sound.

The gods that sleep in museums: the god of fire with his incense burner that resembles an Inquisition tripod; Tlaloc, one of the manifold Gods of the Waters, on his wall of green granite; the Mother Goddess of Waters, the Mother Goddess of Flowers; the immutable expression, echoing from beneath many layers of water, of the Goddess robed in green jade; the enraptured, blissful expression, features crackling with incense, where atoms of sunlight circle—the countenance of the Mother Goddess of Flowers; this world of obligatory servitude in which a stone comes alive when it has been properly carved, the world of organically civilized men whose vital organs too awaken from their slumber, this human world enters into us, participating in the dance of the gods without turning round or looking back, on pain of becoming, like ourselves, crumbled pillars of salt.

In Mexico, since we are talking about Mexico, there is no art: things are made for use. And the world is in perpetual exaltation.

To our disinterested and inert idea of art an authentic culture opposes a violently egoistic and magical, i.e., *interested* idea. For the Mexicans seek contact with the *Manas,* forces latent in every form, unreleased by contemplation of the forms for themselves, but springing to life by magic identification with these forms. And the old Totems are there to hasten the communication.

How hard it is, when everything encourages us to sleep, though we may look about us with conscious, clinging eyes, to wake and yet look about us as in a dream, with eyes that no longer know their function and whose gaze is turned inward.

This is how our strange idea of disinterested action originated, though it is action nonetheless, and all the more violent for skirting the temptation of repose.

Every real effigy has a shadow which is its double; and art must falter and fail from the moment the sculptor believes he has liberated the kind of shadow whose very existence will destroy his repose.

Like all magic cultures expressed by appropriate hieroglyphs, the true theater has its shadows too, and, of all languages and all arts, the theater is the only one left whose shadows have shattered their limitations. From the beginning, one might say its shadows did not tolerate limitations.

Our petrified idea of the theater is connected with our petrified idea of a culture without shadows, where, no matter which way it turns, our mind (*esprit*) encounters only emptiness, though space is full.

But the true theater, because it moves and makes use of living instruments, continues to stir up shadows where life has never ceased to grope its way. The actor does not make the same gestures twice, but he makes gestures, he moves; and although he brutalizes forms, nevertheless behind them and through their destruction he rejoins that which outlives forms and produces their continuation.

The theater, which is in *no thing*, but makes use of everything—gestures, sounds, words, screams, light, darkness— rediscovers itself at precisely the point where the mind requires a language to express its manifestations.

And the fixation of the theater in one language—written words, music, lights, noises—betokens its imminent ruin, the choice of any one language betraying a taste for the special effects of that language; and the dessication of the language accompanies its limitation.

For the theater as for culture, it remains a question of naming and directing shadows: and the theater, not confined to a fixed language and form, not only destroys false shadows but prepares the way for a new generation of shadows, around which assembles the true spectacle of life.

To break through language in order to touch life is to create or recreate the theater; the essential thing is not to believe that this act must remain sacred, i.e., set apart—the essential thing is to believe that not just anyone can create it, and that there must be a preparation.

This leads to the rejection of the usual limitations of man and man's powers, and infinitely extends the frontiers of what is called reality.

We must believe in a sense of life renewed by the theater, a sense of life in which man fearlessly makes himself master of what does not yet exist, and brings it into being. And everything that has not been born can still be brought to life if we are not satisfied to remain mere recording organisms.

Furthermore, when we speak the word "life," it must be understood we are not referring to life as we know it from its surface of fact, but to that fragile, fluctuating center which forms never reach. And if there is still one hellish, truly accursed thing in our time, it is our artistic dallying with forms, instead of being like victims burnt at the stake, signaling through the flames.

# I. The Theater and the Plague

The archives of the little town of Cagliari, in Sardinia, contain the account of an astonishing historical fact.

One night at the end of April or the beginning of May, 1720, about twenty days before the arrival at Marseille of the *Grand-Saint-Antoine*, a vessel whose landing coincided with the most amazing outbreak of the plague in that city's memory, Saint-Rémys, the viceroy of Sardinia, whose reduced monarchical responsibilities had perhaps sensitized him to the most pernicious of viruses, had a particularly afflicting dream: he saw himself infected by the plague he dreamed was ravaging the whole of his tiny state.

Beneath such a scourge, all social forms disintegrate. Order collapses. He observes every infringement of morality, every psychological disaster; he hears his body fluids murmuring within him; torn, failing in a dizzying collapse of tissue, his organs grow heavy and gradually turn to carbon. But is it too late to avert the scourge? Even destroyed, even annihilated, organically pulverized and consumed to his very marrow, he knows we do not die in our dreams, that our will operates even in absurdity, even in the negation of possibility, even in the transmutation of the lies from which truth can be remade.

He wakes up. All these rumors about the plague, these

miasmas of a virus from the Orient:—he will know how to keep them away now.

The *Grand-Saint-Antoine*, a month out of Beirut, asks for permission to dock at Cagliari. The viceroy replies with an insane order, an order considered irresponsible, absurd, idiotic, and despotic by the public and by his own staff. He hastily dispatches the pilot's boat and some men to the ship which he presumes contaminated, with orders that the *Grand-Saint-Antoine* tack about immediately and make full sail away from the town, under threat of being sunk by cannon shot. War against the plague. The autocrat was not going to waste any time.

The particular strength of the influence which this dream exerted upon him should be remarked in passing, since it permitted him, in spite of the sarcasms of the crowd and the skepticism of his followers, to persevere in the ferocity of his orders, trespassing because of it not only upon the rights of man, but upon the simplest respect for human life and upon all sorts of national or international conventions which, in the face of death, are no longer relevant.

In any case, the ship continued on its course, landed at Leghorn, and entered the Marseille roadstead where it was permitted to unload its cargo.

The harbor authorities of Marseille have not kept a record of what happened to its plague-ridden cargo. What became of its crew is more or less known; those who did not die of the plague dispersed to different countries.

The *Grand-Saint-Antoine* did not bring the plague to Marseille. It was already there. And at a point of particular recrudescence. But its centers had been successfully localized.

The plague brought by the *Grand-Saint-Antoine* was the Oriental plague, the original virus, and it is from its approach and diffusion in the city that the particularly dreadful and widespread flaring up of the epidemic dates.

This inspires certain thoughts.

This plague, which seems to reactivate a virus, was of itself capable of inflicting equally virulent damage: of all the crew, the captain alone did not catch the plague; furthermore, it does not appear that the newly arrived victims had ever been in direct contact with the others, confined as they were to close quarters. The *Grand-Saint-Antoine*, which passes within shouting range of Cagliari, in Sardinia, does not deposit the plague there, but the viceroy gathers certain emanations from it in a dream; for it cannot be denied that between the viceroy and the plague a palpable communication, however subtle, was established: and it is too easy and explains nothing to limit the communication of such a disease to contagion by simple contact.

But these relations between Saint-Rémys and the plague, strong enough to liberate themselves as images in his dream, are all the same not strong enough to infect him with the disease.

In any case the town of Cagliari, learning some time later that the ship turned from its shores by the despotic will of its viceroy, its miraculously enlightened viceroy, was at the source of the great epidemic of Marseille, recorded the fact into its archives, where it can be found today.

The plague of 1720 in Marseille has yielded us the only so-called clinical descriptions of the scourge that we possess.

Yet one wonders if the plague described by the Marseille doctors was indeed the same as that of 1347 in Florence which produced the *Decameron*. History, sacred books, among them the Bible, certain old medical treatises describe externally all sorts of plagues concerning which they seem to have paid much less attention to morbid symptoms than to the demoralizing and prodigious effect produced on the victims' minds. They were probably right in doing so. For medicine would have considerable trouble establishing a basic difference between the virus of which Pericles died before Syracuse, supposing the word "virus" to be something other than a mere verbal convenience, and that which manifests its presence in the plague described by Hippocrates, which recent medical treatises regard as a kind of pseudoplague. According to these same treatises, the only authentic plague is the plague from Egypt which rises from the cemeteries uncovered when the Nile recedes. The Bible and Herodotus both call attention to the lightning-like appearance of the plague which in one night decimated the 180,000 men of the Assyrian army, thereby saving the Egyptian empire. If the fact is true, we should have to consider the scourge as the direct instrument or materialization of an intelligent force in close contact with what we call fatality.

And this with or without the army of rats which that same night threw itself upon the Assyrian troops, whose leather armor and harness they gnawed to pieces in a few hours. The fact is comparable to the epidemic which broke out in 660 B.C. in the holy city of Mékao, Japan, on the occasion of a mere change of government.

The plague of 1502 in Provence, which furnished Nostradamus his first opportunities to exercise his powers as a healer, coincided with the most profound political upheavals, downfalls or deaths of kings, disappearance and destruction of provinces, earthquakes, magnetic phenomena of all kinds, exoduses of Jews, which precede or follow, in the political or cosmic order, cataclysms and devastations whose effects those who provoke them are too stupid to foresee and not perverse enough actually to desire.

Whatever may be the errors of historians or physicians concerning the plague, I believe we can agree upon the idea of a malady that would be a kind of psychic entity and would not be carried by a virus. If one wished to analyze closely all the facts of plague contagion that history or even memoirs provide us with, it would be difficult to isolate one actually verified instance of contagion by contact, and Boccaccio's example of swine that died from having sniffed the sheets in which plague victims had been wrapped scarcely suggests more than a kind of mysterious affinity between pig and the nature of the plague, which again would have to be very closely analyzed.

Although there exists no concept of an actual morbid entity, there are some forms upon which the mind can provisionally agree as characterizing certain phenomena, and it seems that the mind can agree to a plague described in the following manner.

Before the onset of any very marked physical or psychological discomfort, the body is covered with red spots, which the victim suddenly notices only when they turn blackish. The victim scarcely hesitates to become alarmed before his head begins to boil and to grow overpoweringly heavy, and he collapses. Then he is seized by a terrible fatigue, the fatigue of a centralized magnetic suction, of his molecules divided and drawn toward their annihilation. His crazed body fluids, unsettled and commingled, seem to be flooding through his flesh. His gorge rises, the inside of his stomach seems as if it were trying to gush out between his teeth. His pulse, which at times slows down to a shadow of itself, a mere virtuality of a pulse, at others races after the boiling of the fever within, consonant with the streaming aberration of his mind, beating in hurried strokes like his heart, which grows intense, heavy, loud; his eyes, first inflamed, then glazed; his swollen gasping tongue, first white, then red, then black, as if charred and split—everything proclaims an unprecedented organic upheaval. Soon the body fluids, furrowed like the earth struck by lightning, like lava kneaded by subterranean forces, search for an outlet. The fieriest point is formed at the center of each spot; around these points the skin rises in blisters like air bubbles under the surface of lava, and these blisters are surrounded by circles, of which the outermost, like Saturn's ring around the incandescent planet, indicates the extreme limit of a bubo.

The body is furrowed with them. But just as volcanoes have their elected spots upon the earth, so bubos make their preferred appearances on the surface of the human body. Around the anus, in the armpits, in the precious places where the active glands faithfully perform their functions, the bubos appear, wherever the organism discharges either its internal rottenness or, according to the case, its life. In most cases a violent burning sensation, localized in one spot, indicates that the organism's life has lost nothing of its force and that a remission of the disease or even its cure is possible. Like silent rage, the most terrible plague is the one that does not reveal its symptoms.

The corpse of a plague victim shows no lesions when opened. The gall bladder, which must filter the heavy and inert wastes of the organism, is full, swollen to bursting with a black, viscous fluid so dense as to suggest a new form of matter altogether. The blood in the arteries and the veins is also black and viscous. The flesh is hard as stone. On the inner surfaces of the stomach membrane, innumerable spurts of blood seem to have appeared. Everything indicates a fundamental disorder in the secretions. But there is neither loss nor destruction of matter, as in leprosy or syphilis. The intestines themselves, which are the site of the bloodiest disorders of all, and in which substances attain an unheard-of degree of putrefaction and petrifaction, are not organically affected. The gall bladder, from which the hardened pus must be virtually torn, as in certain human sacrifices, with a sharp knife, a hard, vitreous instrument of obsidian—the gall bladder is hypertrophied and cracking in places but intact, without any parts missing, without visible lesion, without loss of substance.

In certain cases, however, the injured lungs and brain blacken and grow gangrenous. The softened and pitted lungs fall into chips of some unknown black substance—the brain melts, shrinks, granulates to a sort of coal-black dust.

Two important observations can be made about this fact.

The first is that the plague syndrome is complete without gangrene of the lungs and brain, the victim dying without the putrefaction of any member at all. Without underestimating the nature of the disease, we can say that the organism does not require the presence of a localized physical gangrene to determine its own death.

The second observation is that the only two organs really affected and injured by the plague, the brain and the lungs, are both directly dependent upon the consciousness and the will. We can keep ourselves from breathing or from thinking, can speed up our respiration, give it any rhythm we choose, make it conscious or unconscious at will, introduce a balance between two kinds of breathing: the automatic, which is under the direct control of the sympathetic nervous system, and the other, which is subject to those reflexes of the brain which have once again become conscious.

We can similarly accelerate, retard, and give an arbitrary rhythm to our thinking—can regulate the unconscious play of the mind. We cannot control the filtering of body fluids by the liver or the redistribution of blood by the heart and arteries, cannot restrain the digestion, arrest or accelerate the elimination of matter from the intestine. Thus the plague seems to manifest its presence in and have a preference for the very organs of the body, the particular physical sites, where human will, consciousness, and thought are imminent and apt to occur.

In 1880 or so, a French doctor by the name of Yersin, working on some cadavers of Indo-Chinese natives who had died of the plague, isolated one of those round-headed, short-tailed tadpoles which only the microscope can reveal and called it the plague microbe. Personally, I regard this microbe only as a smaller—infinitely smaller—material element which appears at some moment in the development of the virus, but which in no way accounts for the plague. And I should like this doctor to tell me why all the great plagues, with or without virus, have a duration of five months, after which their virulence abates, and how the Turkish ambassador who was passing through Languedoc towards the end of 1720 was able to draw an imaginary line from Nice through Avignon and Toulouse to Bordeaux, marking the limit of the scourge's geographical extent—a line which events proved to be accurate.

From all this emerges the spiritual physiognomy of a disease whose laws cannot be precisely defined and whose geographical origin it would be idiotic to attempt to determine, for the Egyptian plague is not the Oriental plague, which is not that described by Hippocrates, which is not that of Syracuse, nor of Florence, nor the Black Death which accounted for fifty million lives in medieval Europe. No one can say why the plague strikes the coward who flees it and spares the degenerate who gratifies himself on the corpses. Why distance, chastity, solitude are helpless against the attacks of the scourge; and why a group of debauchees isolating themselves in the country, like Boccaccio with his two well-stocked companions and seven women as lustful as they were religious, can calmly wait for the warm days when the plague withdraws; and why in a nearby castle transformed into a citadel with a cordon of armed men to forbid all entree, the plague turns the garrison and all the occupants into corpses and spares only the armed men exposed to contagion. Who can also explain why the military *cordons sanitaires* which Mehmet Ali established toward the end of the last century, on the occasion of an outbreak of the Egyptian plague, effectively protected convents, schools, prisons, and palaces; and why numerous epidemics of a plague with all the characteristic symptoms of Oriental plague could suddenly break out in medieval Europe in places having no contact whatever with the Orient.

From these peculiarities, these mysteries, these contradictions and these symptoms we must construct the spiritual physiognomy of a disease which progressively destroys the organism like a pain which, as it intensifies and deepens, multiplies its resources and means of access at every level of the sensibility.

But from this spiritual freedom with which the plague develops, without rats, without microbes, and without contact, can be deduced the somber and absolute action of a spectacle which I shall attempt to analyze.

Once the plague is established in a city, the regular forms collapse. There is no maintenance of roads and sewers, no army, no police, no municipal administration. Pyres are lit at random to burn the dead, with whatever means are available. Each family wants to have its own. Then wood, space, and flame itself growing rare, there are family feuds around the pyres, soon followed by a general flight, for the corpses are too numerous. The dead already clog the streets in ragged pyramids gnawed at by animals around the edges. The stench rises in the air like a flame. Entire streets are blocked by the piles of dead. Then the houses open and the delirious victims, their minds crowded with hideous visions, spread howling through the streets. The disease that ferments in their viscera and circulates throughout their entire organism discharges itself in tremendous cerebral explosions. Other victims, without bubos, delirium, pain, or rash, examine themselves proudly in the mirror, in splendid health, as they think, and then fall dead with their shaving mugs in their hands, full of scorn for other victims.

Over the poisonous, thick, bloody streams (color of agony and opium) which gush out of the corpses, strange personages pass, dressed in wax, with noses long as sausages and eyes of glass, mounted on a kind of Japanese sandal made of double wooden tablets, one horizontal, in the form of a sole, the other vertical, to keep them from the contaminated fluids, chanting absurd litanies that cannot prevent them from sinking into the furnace in their turn. These ignorant doctors betray only their fear and their childishness.

The dregs of the population, apparently immunized by their frenzied greed, enter the open houses and pillage riches they know will serve no purpose or profit. And at that moment the theater is born. The theater, i.e., an immediate gratuitousness provoking acts without use or profit.

The last of the living are in a frenzy: the obedient and virtuous son kills his father; the chaste man performs sodomy upon his neighbors. The lecher becomes pure. The miser throws his gold in handfuls out the window. The warrior hero sets fire to the city he once risked his life to save. The dandy decks himself out in his finest clothes and promenades before the charnel houses. Neither the idea of an absence of sanctions nor that of imminent death suffices to motivate acts so gratuitously absurd on the part of men who did not believe death could end anything. And how explain the surge of erotic fever among the recovered victims who, instead of fleeing the city, remain where they are, trying to wrench a criminal pleasure from the dying or even the dead, half crushed under the pile of corpses where chance has lodged them.

But if a mighty scourge is required to make this frenetic gratuitousness show itself, and if this scourge is called the plague, then perhaps we can determine the value of this gratuitousness in relation to our total personality. The state of the victim who dies without material destruction, with all the stigmata of an absolute and almost abstract disease upon him, is identical with the state of an actor entirely penetrated by feelings that do not benefit or even relate to his real condition. Everything in the physical aspect of the actor, as in that of the victim of the plague, shows that life has reacted to the paroxysm, and yet nothing has happened.

Between the victim of the plague who runs in shrieking pursuit of his visions and the actor in pursuit of his feelings;

between the man who invents for himself personages he could never have imagined without the plague, creating them in the midst of an audience of corpses and delirious lunatics and the poet who inopportunely invents characters, entrusting them to a public equally inert or delirious, there are other analogies which confirm the only truths that count and locate the action of the theater like that of the plague on the level of a veritable epidemic.

But whereas the images of the plague, occurring in relation to a powerful state of physical disorganization, are like the last volleys of a spiritual force that is exhausting itself, the images of poetry in the theater are a spiritual force that begins its trajectory in the senses and does without reality altogether. Once launched upon the fury of his task, an actor requires infinitely more power to keep from committing a crime than a murderer needs courage to complete his act, and it is here, in its very gratuitousness, that the action and effect of a feeling in the theater appears infinitely more valid than that of a feeling fulfilled in life.

Compared with the murderer's fury which exhausts itself, that of the tragic actor remains enclosed within a perfect circle. The murderer's fury has accomplished an act, discharges itself, and loses contact with the force that inspired it but can no longer sustain it. That of the actor has taken a form that negates itself to just the degree it frees itself and dissolves into universality.

Extending this spiritual image of the plague, we can comprehend the troubled body fluids of the victim as the material aspect of a disorder which, in other contexts, is equivalent to the conflicts, struggles, cataclysms and debacles our lives afford us. And just as it is not impossible that the unavailing despair of the lunatic screaming in an asylum can cause the plague by a sort of reversibility of feelings and images, one can similarly admit that the external events, political conflicts, natural cataclysms, the order of revolution and the disorder of war, by occurring in the context of the theater, discharge themselves into the sensibility of an audience with all the force of an epidemic.

In *The City of God* St. Augustine complains of this similarity between the action of the plague that kills without destroying the organs and the theater which, without killing, provokes the most mysterious alterations in the mind of not only an individual but an entire populace.

"Know," he says, "you who are ignorant, that these plays, sinful spectacles, were not established in Rome by the vices of men but by the order of your gods. It would be more reasonable to render divine honors unto Scipio[1] than to such gods; surely, they are not worthy of their pontiff! . . .

"In order to appease the plague that killed bodies, your gods commanded in their honor these plays, and your pontiff, wishing to avoid this plague that corrupts souls, opposes the construction of the stage itself. If there still remains among you sufficient trace of intelligence to prefer the soul to the body, choose what deserves your reverence; for the strategy of the evil Spirits, foreseeing that the contagion would end with the body, seized joyfully upon this occasion to introduce a much more dangerous scourge among you, one that attacks not bodies but customs. In fact, such is the blindness, such the corruption produced in the soul by plays that even in these late times those whom this fatal passion possessed, who had escaped from the sack of Rome and taken refuge in Carthage, passed each day at the theater priding themselves on their delirious enthusiasm for the actors."

It is useless to give precise reasons for this contagious delirium. It would be like trying to find reasons why our nervous system after a certain period responds to the vibrations of the subtlest music and is eventually somehow modified by them

[1] Scipio Nasica, grand pontiff, who ordered the theaters of Rome to be leveled and their cellars filled with earth.

in a lasting way. First of all we must recognize that the theater, like the plague, is a delirium and is communicative.

The mind believes what it sees and does what it believes: that is the secret of the fascination. Nor does Saint Augustine's text question for one moment the reality of this fascination.

However, there are conditions to be rediscovered in order to engender in the mind a spectacle capable of fascinating it: and this is not a simple matter of art.

For if the theater is like the plague, it is not only because it affects important collectivities and upsets them in an identical way. In the theater as in the plague there is something both victorious and vengeful: we are aware that the spontaneous conflagration which the plague lights wherever it passes is nothing else than an immense liquidation.

A social disaster so far-reaching, an organic disorder so mysterious—this overflow of vices, this total exorcism which presses and impels the soul to its utmost—all indicate the presence of a state which is nevertheless characterized by extreme strength and in which all the powers of nature are freshly discovered at the moment when something essential is going to be accomplished.

The plague takes images that are dormant, a latent disorder, and suddenly extends them into the most extreme gestures; the theater also takes gestures and pushes them as far as they will go: like the plague it reforges the chain between what is and what is not, between the virtuality of the possible and what already exists in materialized nature. It recovers the notion of symbols and archetypes which act like silent blows, rests, leaps of the heart, summons of the lymph, inflammatory images thrust into our abruptly wakened heads. The theater restores us all our dormant conflicts and all their powers, and gives these powers names we hail as symbols: and behold! before our eyes is fought a battle of symbols, one charging against another in an impossible melée; for there can be theater only from the moment when the impossible really begins and when the poetry which occurs on the stage sustains and superheats the realized symbols.

These symbols, the sign of ripe powers previously held in servitude and unavailable to reality, burst forth in the guise of incredible images which give freedom of the city and of existence to acts that are by nature hostile to the life of societies.

In the true theater a play disturbs the senses' repose, frees the repressed unconscious, incites a kind of virtual revolt (which moreover can have its full effect only if it remains virtual), and imposes on the assembled collectivity an attitude that is both difficult and heroic.

Thus in Ford's *'Tis Pity She's a Whore*, from the moment the curtain rises, we see to our utter stupefaction a creature flung into an insolent vindication of incest, exerting all the vigor of his youthful consciousness to proclaim and justify it.

He does not waver an instant, does not hesitate a minute, and thereby shows of how little account are all the barriers that could be opposed to him. He is heroically criminal and audaciously, ostentatiously heroic. Everything drives him in this direction and inflames his enthusiasm; he recognizes neither earth nor heaven, only the force of his convulsive passion, to which the rebellious and equally heroic passion of Annabella does not fail to respond.

"I weep," she says, "not with remorse but for fear I shall not be able to satisfy my passion." They are both forgers, hypocrites, and liars for the sake of their superhuman passion which laws obstruct and condemn but which they will put beyond the law.

Vengeance for vengeance, and crime for crime. When we believe them threatened, hunted down, lost, when we are ready to pity them as victims, then they reveal themselves ready to render destiny threat for threat and blow for blow.

With them we proceed from excess to excess and vindication to vindication. Annabella is captured, convicted of adultery and incest, trampled upon, insulted, dragged by the hair, and we are astonished to discover that far from seeking a means of escape, she provokes her executioner still further and sings out in a kind of obstinate heroism. It is the absolute condition of revolt, it is an exemplary case of love without respite which makes us, the spectators, gasp with anguish at the idea that nothing will ever be able to stop it.

If we desire an example of absolute freedom in revolt, Ford's Annabella provides this poetic example bound up with the image of absolute danger.

And when we tell ourselves we have reached the paroxysm of horror, blood, and flouted laws, of poetry which consecrates revolt, we are obliged to advance still further into an endless vertigo.

But ultimately, we tell ourselves, there is vengeance, there is death for such audacity and such irresistible crime.

But there is no such thing. Giovanni, the lover, inspired by the passion of a great poet, puts himself beyond vengeance, beyond crime, by still another crime, one that is indescribably passionate; beyond threats, beyond horror by an even greater horror, one which overthrows at one and the same time law, morality, and all those who dare set themselves up as administrators of justice.

A trap is cleverly set, a great banquet is given where, among the guests, hired ruffians and spies are to be hidden, ready at the first signal to throw themselves upon him. But this hero, cornered, lost, and inspired by love, will let no one pass sentence on this love.

You want, he seems to say, my love's flesh and blood. Very well, I will throw this love in your face and shower you with its blood—for you are incapable of rising to its height!

And he kills his beloved and tears out her heart as if to feast upon it in the middle of a banquet where he himself is the one whom the guests had hoped to devour.

And before being executed, he manages to kill his rival,

his sister's husband, who has dared to come between him and his love, and despatches him in a final combat which then appears as his own spasm of agony.

Like the plague, the theater is a formidable call to the forces that impel the mind by example to the source of its conflicts. And it is evident that Ford's passional example merely symbolizes a still greater and absolutely essential task.

The terrorizing apparition of Evil which in the Mysteries of Eleusis was produced in its pure, truly revealed form corresponds to the dark hour of certain ancient tragedies which all true theater must recover.

If the essential theater is like the plague, it is not because it is contagious, but because like the plague it is the revelation, the bringing forth, the exteriorization of a depth of latent cruelty by means of which all the perverse possibilities of the mind, whether of an individual or a people, are localized.

Like the plague the theater is the time of evil, the triumph of dark powers that are nourished by a power even more profound until extinction.

In the theater as in the plague there is a kind of strange sun, a light of abnormal intensity by which it seems that the difficult and even the impossible suddenly become our normal element. And Ford's play, like all true theater, is within the radiance of this strange sun. His Annabella resembles the plague's freedom by means of which, from degree to degree, stage to stage, the victim swells his individuality and the survivor gradually becomes a grandiose and overwhelming being.

We can now say that all true freedom is dark, and infallibly identified with sexual freedom which is also dark, although we do not know precisely why. For it has been a long time since the Platonic Eros, the procreative sense, the freedom of life vanished beneath the somber veneer of the *Libido* which is identified with all that is dirty, abject, infamous in the process of living and of throwing oneself headlong with a natural and impure vigor, with a perpetually renewed strength, upon life.

And that is why all the great Myths are dark, so that one cannot imagine, save in an atmosphere of carnage, torture, and bloodshed, all the magnificent Fables which recount to the multitudes the first sexual division and the first carnage of essences that appeared in creation.

The theater, like the plague, is in the image of this carnage and this essential separation. It releases conflicts, disengages powers, liberates possibilities, and if these possibilities and these powers are dark, it is the fault not of the plague nor of the theater, but of life.

We do not see that life as it is and as it has been fashioned for us provides many reasons for exaltation. It appears that by means of the plague, a gigantic abscess, as much moral as social, has been collectively drained; and that like the plague, the theater has been created to drain abscesses collectively.

Perhaps the theater's poison, injected into the social body, disintegrates it, as Saint Augustine says, but at least it does so as a plague, as an avenging scourge, a redeeming epidemic in which credulous ages have chosen to see the finger of God and which is nothing but the application of a law of nature whereby every gesture is counterbalanced by a gesture and every action by its reaction.

The theater like the plague is a crisis which is resolved by death or cure. And the plague is a superior disease because it is a total crisis after which nothing remains except death or an extreme purification. Similarly the theater is a disease because it is the supreme equilibrium which cannot be achieved without destruction. It invites the mind to share a delirium which exalts its energies; and we can see, to conclude, that from the human point of view, the action of theater, like that of plague, is beneficial, for, impelling men to see themselves as they are, it causes the mask to fall, reveals the lie, the slackness, baseness, and hypocrisy of our world; it shakes off the asphyxiating inertia of matter which invades even the clearest testimony of the senses; and in revealing to collectivities of men their dark power, their hidden force, it invites them to take, in the face of destiny, a superior and heroic attitude they would never have assumed without it.

And the question we must now ask is whether, in this slippery world which is committing suicide without noticing it, there can be found a nucleus of men capable of imposing this superior notion of the theater, men who will restore to all of us the natural and magic equivalent of the dogmas in which we no longer believe.

## II. Metaphysics and the Mise en Scène

In the Louvre there is a work by a primitive painter, known or unknown I cannot say, but whose name will never be representative of an important period in the history of art. This painter is Lucas van den Leyden and in my opinion he makes the four or five centuries of painting that come after him inane and useless. The canvas I speak of is entitled "The Daughters of Lot," a biblical subject in the style of the period. Of course the Bible in the Middle Ages was not understood in the same way we understand it today, and this canvas is a curious example of the mystic deductions that can be derived from it. Its emotion, in any case, is visible even from a distance; it affects the mind with an almost thunderous visual harmony, intensely active throughout the painting, yet to be gathered from a single glance. Even before you can discern what is going on, you sense something tremendous happening in the painting, and the ear, one would say, is as moved by it as the eye. A drama of high intellectual importance seems massed there like a sudden gathering of clouds which the wind or some much more direct fatality has impelled together to measure their thunderbolts.

The sky of the picture, in fact, is black and swollen; but even before we can tell that the drama was born in the sky, was happening in the sky, the peculiar lighting of the canvas, the jumble of shapes, the impression the whole gives at a distance—everything betokens a kind of drama of nature for which I defy any painter of the Great Periods to give us an equivalent.

A tent is pitched at the sea's edge, in front of which Lot is sitting, wearing full armor and a handsome red beard, watching his daughters parade up and down as if he were a guest at a prostitutes' banquet.

And in fact they are strutting about, some as mothers of families, others as amazons, combing their hair and fencing, as if they had never had any other purpose than to charm their father, to be his plaything or his instrument. We are thus presented with the profoundly incestuous character of the old theme which the painter develops here in passionate images. Its profound sexuality is proof that the painter has understood his subject absolutely as a modern man, that is, as we ourselves would understand it: proof that its character of profound but poetic sexuality has escaped him no more than it has eluded us.

On the left of the picture, and a little to the rear, a black tower rises to prodigious heights, supported at its base by a whole system of rocks, plants, zigzagging roads marked with milestones and dotted here and there with houses. And by a happy effect of perspective, one of these roads at a certain point disengages itself from the maze through which it has been creeping, crosses a bridge, and at last receives a ray of that stormy light which brims over between the clouds and showers the region irregularly. The sea in the background of the canvas is extremely high, at the same time extremely calm considering the fiery skein that is boiling up in one corner of the sky.

It happens that when we are watching fireworks, the crackling nocturnal bombardment of shooting stars, sky rockets, and Roman candles may reveal to our eyes in its hallucinatory light certain details of landscape, wrought in relief against the night: trees, towers, mountains, houses, whose lighting and sudden apparition will always remain definitely linked in our minds with the idea of this noisy rending of the darkness. There is no better way of expressing this submission of the different elements of landscape to the fire revealed in the sky of this painting than by saying that even though they possess their own light, they remain in spite of everything related to this sudden fire as dim echoes, living points of reference born from it and placed where they are to permit it to exercise its full destructive force.

There is moreover something frighteningly energetic and troubling in the way the painter depicts this fire, like an element still active and in motion, yet with an immobilized expression. It matters little how this effect is obtained, it is real; it is enough to see the canvas to be convinced of it.

In any case, this fire, which no one will deny produces an impression of intelligence and malice, serves, by its very violence, as a counterbalance in the mind to the heavy material stability of the rest of the painting.

Between the sea and the sky, but towards the right, and on the same level in perspective as the Black Tower, projects a thin spit of land crowned by a monastery in ruins.

This spit of land, so close that it is visible from the shore where Lot's tent stands, reveals behind it an immense gulf in which an unprecedented naval disaster seems to have occurred. Vessels cut in two and not yet sunk lean upon the sea as upon crutches, strewing everywhere their uprooted masts and spars.

It would be difficult to say why the impression of disaster, which is created by the sight of only one or two ships in pieces, is so complete.

It seems as if the painter possessed certain secrets of linear harmony, certain means of making that harmony affect the brain directly, like a physical agent. In any case this impression of intelligence prevailing in external nature and especially in the manner of its representation is apparent in several other details of the canvas, witness for example the bridge as high as an eight-story house standing out against the sea, across which people are filing, one after another, like Ideas in Plato's cave.

It would be untrue to claim that the ideas which emerge from this picture are clear. They are however of a grandeur that painting which is merely painting, i.e., all painting for several centuries, has completely abandoned: we are not accustomed to it.

In addition, Lot and his daughters suggest an idea concerning sexuality and reproduction, for Lot is seemingly placed there among his daughters to profit unfairly by them, like a drone.

It is almost the only social idea that the painting contains.

All the other ideas are metaphysical. I am sorry to use this word, but it is their name; and I shall even say that their poetic grandeur, their concrete efficacity upon us, is a result of their being metaphysical; their spiritual profundity is inseparable from the formal and exterior harmony of the picture.

There is, again, an idea of Becoming which the various details of the landscape and the way they are painted—the way their planes and perspectives are blotted out or made to correspond—introduce into our minds with precisely the effect of a piece of music.

There is another idea, of Fatality, expressed less by the sudden apparition of this fire, than by the solemn way in which all the forms are organized or disorganized beneath it, some as if bent under a wind of irresistible panic, others immobile and almost ironic, all obeying a powerful intellectual harmony, which seems to be the exteriorization of the very spirit of nature.

And there is an idea of Chaos, an idea of the Marvelous, an idea of Equilibrium; there are even one or two concerning the impotence of Speech whose uselessness this supremely material and anarchic painting seems to demonstrate.

I say in any case that this painting is what the theater should be, if it knew how to speak the language that belongs to it.

And I ask this question:

How does it happen that in the theater, at least in the theater as we know it in Europe, or better in the Occident, everything specifically theatrical, i.e., everything that cannot be expressed in speech, in words, or, if you prefer, everything that is not contained in the dialogue (and the dialogue itself considered as a function of its possibilities for "sound" on the stage, as a function of the *exigencies* of this sonorisation) is left in the background?

How does it happen, moreover, that the Occidental theater (I say Occidental because there are fortunately others, like the Oriental theater, which have preserved intact the idea of theater, while in the Occident this idea—like all the rest—has been *prostituted*), how does it happen that the Occidental theater does not see theater under any other aspect than as a theater of dialogue?

Dialogue—a thing written and spoken—does not belong specifically to the stage, it belongs to books, as is proved by the fact that in all handbooks of literary history a place is reserved for the theater as a subordinate branch of the history of the spoken language.

I say that the stage is a concrete physical place which asks to be filled, and to be given its own concrete language to speak.

I say that this concrete language, intended for the senses and independent of speech, has first to satisfy the senses, that there is a poetry of the senses as there is a poetry of language, and that this concrete physical language to which I refer is truly theatrical only to the degree that the thoughts it expresses are beyond the reach of the spoken language.

I will be asked what these thoughts are which words cannot express and which, far more than words, would find their ideal expression in the concrete physical language of the stage.

I will answer this question a little later.

What is essential now, it seems to me, is to determine what this physical language consists of, this solidified, materialized language by means of which theater is able to differentiate itself from speech.

It consists of everything that occupies the stage, everything that can be manifested and expressed materially on a stage and that is addressed first of all to the senses instead of being addressed primarily to the mind as is the language of words. (I am well aware that words too have possibilities as sound, different ways of being projected into space, which are called *intonations*. Furthermore, there would be a great deal to say about the concrete value of intonation in the theater, about this faculty words have of creating a music in their own right according to the way they are pronounced, independently of their concrete meaning and even going counter to this meaning—of creating beneath language a subterranean current of impressions, correspondences, and analogies; but this theatrical consideration of language is already a subordinate *aspect* of language for the playwright, an accessory consideration of which, especially in our time, he takes no account in the construction of his plays. So let us pass on.)

This language created for the senses must from the outset be concerned with satisfying them. This does not prevent it from developing later its full intellectual effect on all possible levels and in every direction. But it permits the substitution, for the poetry of language, of a poetry in space which will be resolved in precisely the domain which does not belong strictly to words.

Doubtless you would prefer, for a better understanding of what I mean, a few examples of this poetry in space capable of creating kinds of material images equivalent to word images. You will find these examples a little further on.

This very difficult and complex poetry assumes many aspects: especially the aspects of all the means of expression utilizable on the stage,[1] such as music, dance, plastic art, pantomime, mimicry, gesticulation, intonation, architecture, lighting, and scenery.

Each of these means has its own intrinsic poetry, and a kind of ironic poetry as well, resulting from the way it combines with the other means of expression; and the consequences of these combinations, of their reactions and their reciprocal destructions, are easy to perceive.

I shall return a little later to this poetry which can be fully effective only if it is concrete, i.e., only if it produces something objectively from the fact of its *active* presence on the stage;—only if a sound, as in the Balinese theater, has its equivalent in a gesture and, instead of serving as a decoration, an accompaniment of a thought, instead causes its movement, directs it, destroys it, or changes it completely, etc.

One form of this poetry in space—besides the one that can be created by combinations of lines, shapes, colors, objects in their natural state, such as one finds in all the arts— belongs to sign-language. I hope I shall be allowed to speak for a moment about this other aspect of pure theatrical language which does without words, a language of signs, gestures and attitudes having an ideographic value as they exist in certain unperverted pantomimes.

By "unperverted pantomime" I mean direct Pantomime where gestures—instead of representing words or sentences,

[1] To the degree that they prove capable of profiting from the immediate physical possibilities the stage offers them in order to substitute, for fixed forms of art, living and intimidating forms by which the sense of old ceremonial magic can find a new reality in the theater; to the degree that they yield to what might be called the *physical temptation* of the stage.

as in our European Pantomime (a mere fifty years old!)
which is merely a distortion of the mute roles of Italian
comedy—represent ideas, attitudes of mind, aspects of nature, all in an effective, concrete manner, i.e., by constantly
evoking objects or natural details, like that Oriental language
which represents night by a tree on which a bird that has
already closed one eye is beginning to close the other. Another
such abstract idea or attitude of mind could be represented
by some of the innumerable symbols from Scripture, as the
needle's eye through which the camel cannot pass.

It is plain that these signs constitute true hieroglyphs, in
which man, to the extent that he contributes to their formation, is only a form like the rest, yet to which, because of his
double nature, he adds a singular prestige.

This language which evokes in the mind images of an intense natural (or spiritual) poetry provides a good idea of
what a poetry in space independent of spoken language could
mean in the theater.

Whatever the case of this language and its poetry may be,
I have noticed that in our theater which lives under the exclusive dictatorship of speech, this language of gesture and
mime, this wordless pantomime, these postures, attitudes,
objective intonations, in brief everything I consider specifically
theatrical in the theater, all these elements when they exist
apart from text are generally considered the minor part of
theater; they are negligently referred to as "craft," and identified with what is understood by staging or "production," and
can consider themselves fortunate if the words *mise en scène*
are not applied to the idea of artistic and external sumptuousness pertaining exclusively to costumes, lighting, and set.

And in opposition to this way of looking at things, a way
which seems to me entirely Occidental or rather Latin, i.e.,
pigheaded, I shall say that to the degree that this language
derives from the stage, draws its efficacity from its spontaneous creation on the stage, to the degree that it struggles di-

rectly with the stage without passing through words (and why
not conceive of a play composed directly on the stage, realized
on the stage)—it is the *mise en scène* that is the theater much
more than the written and spoken play. I will be asked no
doubt to define what is Latin in this way of seeing opposed to
mine. What is Latin is this need to use words to express ideas
that are obvious. For to me obvious ideas are, in the theater
as everywhere else, dead and done with.

The idea of a play made directly in terms of the stage, en-
countering obstacles of both production and performance,
compels the discovery of an active language, active and anarchic, a language in which the customary limits of feelings
and words are transcended.

In any case, and I hasten to say it at once, a theater which
subordinates the *mise en scène* and production, i.e., everything
in itself that is specifically theatrical, to the text, is a theater
of idiots, madmen, inverts, grammarians, grocers, antipoets
and positivists, i.e., Occidentals.

Furthermore, I am well aware that the language of gestures
and postures, dance and music, is less capable of analyzing
a character, revealing a man's thoughts, or elucidating states
of consciousness clearly and precisely than is verbal language,
but who ever said the theater was created to analyze a character, to resolve the conflicts of love and duty, to wrestle with
all the problems of a topical and psychological nature that
monopolize our contemporary stage?

Given the theater as we see it here, one would say there
is nothing more to life than knowing whether we can make
love skillfully, whether we will go to war or are cowardly
enough to make peace, how we cope with our little pangs of
conscience, and whether we will become conscious of our
"complexes" (in the language of experts) or if indeed our
"complexes" will do us in. Rarely, moreover, does the debate
rise to a social level, rarely do we question our social and
moral system. Our theater never goes so far as to ask whether

this social and moral system might not by chance be iniquitous.

I believe, however, that our present social state is iniquitous
and should be destroyed. If this is a fact for the theater to be
preoccupied with, it is even more a matter for machine guns.
Our theater is not even capable of asking the question in the
burning and effective way it must be asked, but even if it
should ask this question it would still be far from its purpose,
which is for me a higher and more secret one.

All the preoccupations enumerated above stink unbeliev-
ably of man, provisional, material man, I shall even say
*carrion man*. Such preoccupation with personal problems disgusts me, and disgusts me all the more with nearly the whole
contemporary theater which, as human as it is antipoetic,
except for three or four plays, seems to me to stink of deca-
dence and pus.

The contemporary theater is decadent because it has lost
the feeling on the one hand for seriousness and on the other
for laughter; because it has broken away from gravity, from
effects that are immediate and painful—in a word, from
Danger.

Because it has lost a sense of real humor, a sense of laughter's power of physical and anarchic dissociation.

Because it has broken away from the spirit of profound
anarchy which is at the root of all poetry.

It must be admitted that everything in the destination of
an object, in the meaning or the use of a natural form, is a
matter of convention.

Nature, in giving a tree the form of a tree, could just as
well have given it the form of an animal or of a hill; we would
have thought *tree* for the animal or the hill, and the trick
would have been turned.

It is agreed that a beautiful woman has a melodious voice;
if, since the world began, we had heard all beautiful women

call to us in trumpet blasts and greet us like bellowing elephants, we would have eternally associated the idea of bellowing with the idea of a beautiful woman, and a portion of our inner vision of the world would have been radically transformed thereby.

This helps us to understand that poetry is anarchic to the degree that it brings into play all the relationships of object to object and of form to signification. It is anarchic also to the degree that its occurrence is the consequence of a disorder that draws us closer to chaos.

I shall give no further examples. One could multiply them infinitely and not only with humorous ones like those I have just used.

Theatrically these inversions of form, displacements of signification could become the essential element of that humorous poetry in space which is the exclusive province of the *mise en scène.*

In a Marx Brothers' film a man thinks he is going to take a woman in his arms but instead gets a cow, which moos. And through a conjunction of circumstances which it would take too long to analyze here, that moo, at just that moment, assumes an intellectual dignity equal to any woman's cry.

Such a situation, possible in the cinema, is no less possible in the theater as it exists: it would take very little—for instance, replace the cow with an animated manikin, a kind of monster endowed with speech, or a man disguised as an animal—to rediscover the secret of an objective poetry at the root of humor, which the theater has renounced and abandoned to the Music Hall, and which the Cinema later adopted.

A moment ago I mentioned danger. The best way, it seems to me, to realize this idea of danger on the stage is by the *objective* unforeseen, the unforeseen not in situations but in things, the abrupt, untimely transition from an intellectual image to a true image; for example, a man who is blaspheming sees suddenly and realistically materialized before him the image of his blasphemy (always on condition, I would add, that such an image is not entirely gratuitous but engenders in its turn other images in the same spiritual vein, etc.).

Another example would be the sudden appearance of a fabricated Being, made of wood and cloth, entirely invented, corresponding to nothing, yet disquieting by nature, capable of reintroducing on the stage a little breath of that great metaphysical fear which is at the root of all ancient theater.

The Balinese with their imaginary dragon, like all the Orientals, have not lost the sense of that mysterious fear which they know is one of the most stirring (and indeed essential) elements of the theater when it is restored to its proper level.

True poetry is, willy nilly, metaphysical and it is just its metaphysical bearing, I should say, the intensity of its metaphysical effect, that comprises its essential worth.

This is the second or third time I have brought up metaphysics here. I was speaking, a moment ago, apropos of psychology, about dead ideas, and I expect many will be tempted to tell me that if there is one inhuman idea in the world, one ineffectual and dead idea which conveys little enough even to the mind, it is indeed the idea of metaphysics.

This is due, as René Guénon says, "to our purely Occidental way, our antipoetic and truncated way of considering principles (apart from the massive and energetic spiritual state which corresponds to them)."

In the Oriental theater of metaphysical tendencies, as opposed to the Occidental theater of psychological tendencies, this whole complex of gestures, signs, postures, and sonorities which constitute the language of stage performance, this language which develops all its physical and poetic effects on every level of consciousness and in all the senses, necessarily induces thought to adopt profound attitudes which could be called *metaphysics-in-action*.

I shall take up this point again in a moment. For the present let us return to the theater as we know it.

A few days ago, I was present at a discussion about the theater. I saw some sort of human snakes, otherwise known as playwrights, explain how to worm a play into the good graces of a director, like certain men in history who used to insinuate poison into the ears of their rivals. There was some question, I believe, of determining the future orientation of the theater and, in other terms, its destiny.

No one determined anything, and at no time was there any question of the true destiny of the theater, i.e., of what, by definition and essence, the theater is destined to represent, nor of the means at its disposal for realizing this destiny. On the contrary the theater seemed to me a sort of frozen world, its artists cramped among gestures that will never be good for anything again, brittle intonations which are already falling to pieces, music reduced to a kind of arithmetic whose figures are beginning to fade, some sort of luminous explosions, themselves congealed and responding to vague traces of movement—and around all this an extraordinary fluttering of men in black suits who quarrel over the receipts, at the threshold of a white-hot box office. As if the theatrical mechanism were henceforth reduced to all that surrounds it; and because it is reduced to what surrounds it and because the theater is reduced to everything that is not the theater, its atmosphere stinks in the nostrils of people of taste.

For me the theater is identical with its possibilities for realization when the most extreme poetic results are derived from them; the possibilities for realization in the theater relate entirely to the *mise en scène* considered as a language in space and in movement.

To derive, then, the most extreme poetic results from the means of realization is to make metaphysics of them, and I think no one will object to this way of considering the question.

And to make metaphysics out of language, gestures, attitudes, sets, and music from a theatrical point of view is, it seems to me, to consider them in relation to all the ways they can have of making contact with time and with movement.

To give objective examples of this poetry that follows upon the way a gesture, a sonority, an intonation presses with more or less insistence upon this or that segment of space at such and such a time appears to me as difficult as to communicate in words the feeling of a particular sound or the degree and quality of a physical pain. It depends upon the production and can be determined only on the stage.

I should now review all the means of expression which the theater (or the *mise en scène*, which, in the system I have just expounded, is identified with it) contains. That would carry me too far, and I shall simply select from them one or two examples.

First, the spoken language.

To make metaphysics out of a spoken language is to make the language express what it does not ordinarily express: to make use of it in a new, exceptional, and unaccustomed fashion; to reveal its possibilities for producing physical shock; to divide and distribute it actively in space; to deal with intonations in an absolutely concrete manner, restoring their power to shatter as well as really to manifest something; to turn against language and its basely utilitarian, one could say alimentary, sources, against its trapped-beast origins; and finally, to consider language as the form of *Incantation*.

Everything in this active poetic mode of envisaging expression on the stage leads us to abandon the modern humanistic and psychological meaning of the theater, in order to recover the religious and mystic preference of which our theater has completely lost the sense.

If it is enough to pronounce the words *religious* or *mystic* to be taken for a churchwarden or an illiterate priest outside a Buddhist temple, at best good only for turning prayer wheels, this merely signifies and condemns our incapacity to derive the full import from our words and our profound ignorance of the spirit of synthesis and analogy.

Perhaps it means that at the point where we are we have lost all touch with the true theater, since we confine it to the domain of what daily thought can reach, the familiar or unfamiliar domain of consciousness;—and if we address ourselves theatrically to the unconscious, it is merely to take from it what it has been able to collect (or conceal) of accessible everyday experience.

Let it be further said that one of the reasons for the physical efficacity upon the mind, for the force of the direct images of action in certain productions of the Oriental theater, such as those of the Balinese theater, is that this theater is based upon age-old traditions which have preserved intact the secrets of using gestures, intonations, and harmonies in relation to the senses and on all possible levels—this does not condemn the Oriental theater, but it condemns us, and along with us the state of things in which we live and which is to be destroyed, destroyed with diligence and malice on every level and at every point where it prevents the free exercise of thought.

## III. The Alchemical Theater

There is a mysterious identity of essence between the principle of the theater and that of alchemy. For like alchemy, the theater, considered from the point of view of its deepest principle, is developed from a certain number of fundamentals which are the same for all the arts and which aim on the spiritual and imaginary level at an efficacity analogous to the process which in the physical world actually turns all matter into gold. But there is a still deeper resemblance between the theater and alchemy, one which leads much further metaphysically. It is that alchemy and the theater are so to speak virtual arts, and do not carry their end—or their reality—within themselves.

Where alchemy, through its symbols, is the spiritual Double of an operation which functions only on the level of real matter, the theater must also be considered as the Double, not of this direct, everyday reality of which it is gradually being reduced to a mere inert replica—as empty as it is sugar-coated—but of another archetypal and dangerous reality, a reality of which the Principles, like dolphins, once they have shown their heads, hurry to dive back into the obscurity of the deep.

For this reality is not human but inhuman, and man with his customs and his character counts for very little in it. Perhaps even man's head would not be left to him if he were to confide himself to this reality—and even so it would have to be an absolutely stripped, malleable, and organic head, in which just enough formal matter would remain so that the principles might exert their effects within it in a completely physical way.

Before going further, let us consider the curious predilection for the theatrical vocabulary of all books dealing with alchemical subjects, as if their authors had sensed from the beginning all that was *representative*, i.e., theatrical, in the whole series of *symbols* by means of which the Great Work is to be realized spiritually, while waiting for it to be realized actually and materially, as well as in the digressions and errors of the ill-informed mind among these operations, in the almost "dialectical" sequence of all the aberrations, phantasms, mirages, and hallucinations which those who attempt to perform these operations *by purely human means* cannot fail to encounter.

All true alchemists know that the alchemical symbol is a mirage as the theater is a mirage. And this perpetual allusion to the materials and the principle of the theater found in almost all alchemical books should be understood as the expression of an identity (of which alchemists are extremely aware) existing between the world in which the characters, objects, images, and in a general way all that constitutes the *virtual reality* of the theater develops, and the purely fictitious and illusory world in which the symbols of alchemy are evolved.

These symbols, which indicate what might be called philosophical states of matter, already start the mind on its way toward that fiery purification, that unification and that emaciation (in a horribly simplified and pure sense) of the natural molecules; on its way toward that operation which permits, by sheer force of destructive analysis, the reconception and reconstitution of solids according that equilibrium of spiritual descent by which they ultimately become gold again. It is not sufficiently understood how much the material symbolism used to designate this mysterious operation corresponds to a parallel symbolism in the mind, a deployment of ideas and appearances by which all that is theatrical in the theater is designated and can be distinguished philosophically.

Let me explain. Perhaps it has already been understood that the genre of theater to which I refer has nothing to do with the kind of realistic, social theater which changes with each historical period and in which the ideas that animated the theater at its origin can no longer be discerned except as caricatures of gestures, unrecognizable because their intention has changed so greatly. Like words themselves, the ideas of the archetypal, primitive theater have in time ceased to generate an image, and instead of being a means of expansion are only an impasse, a mausoleum of the mind.

Perhaps before proceeding further I shall be asked to define what I mean by the archetypal, primitive theater. And we shall thereby approach the very heart of the matter.

If in fact we raise the question of the origins and *raison d'être* (or primordial necessity) of the theater, we find, metaphysically, the materialization or rather the exteriorization of a kind of essential drama which would contain, in a manner at once manifold and unique, the essential principles of all drama, already *disposed* and *divided,* not so much as to lose their character as principles, but enough to comprise, in a substantial and active fashion (i.e., resonantly), an infinite perspective of conflicts. To analyze such a drama philosophically is impossible; only poetically and by seizing upon what is communicative and magnetic in the principles of all the arts can we, by shapes, sounds, music, and volumes, evoke, passing by way of all natural resemblances of images and affinities to each other not the primordial directions of the mind, which our excessive logical intellectualism would reduce to merely useless schemata, but states of an acuteness so intense and so absolute that we sense, beyond the tremors of all music and form, the underlying menace of a chaos as decisive as it is dangerous.

And this essential drama, we come to realize, exists, and in the image of something subtler than Creation itself, something which must be represented as the result of one Will alone—and *without conflict.*

We must believe that the essential drama, the one at the root of all the Great Mysteries, is associated with the second phase of Creation, that of difficulty and of the Double, that of matter and the materialization of the idea.

It seems indeed that where simplicity and order reign, there can be no theater nor drama, and the true theater, like poetry as well, though by other means, is born out of a kind of organized anarchy after philosophical battles which are the passionate aspect of these primitive unifications.

Now these conflicts which the Cosmos in turmoil offers us in a philosophically distorted and impure manner, alchemy offers us in all their rigorous intellectuality, since it permits us to attain once more to the sublime, *but with drama,* after a meticulous and unremitting pulverization of every insufficiently fine, insufficiently matured form, since it follows from the very principle of alchemy not to let the spirit take its leap until it has passed through all the filters and foundations of existing matter, and to redouble this labor at the incandescent edges of the future. For it might be said that in order to merit material gold, the mind must first prove that it was capable of the other kind, that it would have earned it, would have attained to it, only by assenting to it, by seeing it as a secondary symbol of the fall it must experience in order to rediscover in solid and opaque form the expression of light itself, of rarity, and of irreducibility.

The theatrical operation of making gold, by the immensity of the conflicts it provokes, by the prodigious number of forces

it throws one against the other and rouses, by this appeal to
a sort of essential redistillation brimming with consequences
and surcharged with spirituality, ultimately evokes in the
spirit an absolute and abstract purity, beyond which there
can be nothing, and which can be conceived as a unique
sound, defining note, caught on the wing, the organic part of
an indescribable vibration.

The Orphic Mysteries which subjugated Plato must have
possessed on the moral and psychological level something of
this definitive and transcendent aspect of the *alchemical theater*, with elements of an extraordinary psychological density,
and conversely must have evoked the symbols of alchemy,
which provide the spiritual means of decanting and trans-
fusing matter, must have evoked the passionate and decisive
transfusion of matter by mind.

We are told that the Mysteries of Eleusis confined themselves to the *mise en scène* of a certain number of moral
truths. I believe instead that they must have consisted of pro-
jections and precipitations of conflicts, indescribable battles of
principles joined from that dizzying and slippery perspective
in which every truth is lost in the realization of the inextricable and unique fusion of the abstract and the concrete, and
I think that by the music of instruments, the combinations of
colors and shapes, of which we have lost every notion, they
must have brought to a climax that nostalgia for pure beauty
of which Plato, at least once in this world, must have found
the complete, sonorous, streaming naked realization: to resolve by conjunctions unimaginably strange to our waking
minds, to resolve or even annihilate every conflict produced
by the antagonism of matter and mind, idea and form, concrete and abstract, and to dissolve all appearances into one
unique expression which must have been the equivalent of
spiritualized gold.

# IV. On the Balinese Theater

The spectacle of the Balinese theater, which draws upon dance, song, pantomime—and a little of the theater as we understand it in the Occident—restores the theater, by means of ceremonies of indubitable age and well-tried efficacity, to its original destiny which it presents as a combination of all these elements fused together in a perspective of hallucination and fear.

It is very remarkable that the first of the little plays which compose this spectacle, in which we are shown a father's remonstrances to his tradition-flouting daughter, begins with an entrance of phantoms; the male and female characters who will develop a dramatic but familiar subject appear to us first in their spectral aspect and are seen in that hallucinatory perspective appropriate to every theatrical character, before the situations in this kind of symbolic sketch are allowed to develop. Here indeed situations are only a pretext. The drama does not develop as a conflict of feelings but as a conflict of spiritual states, themselves ossified and transformed into gestures—diagrams. In a word, the Balinese have realized, with the utmost rigor, the idea of pure theater, where everything, conception and realization alike, has value, has existence only in proportion to its degree of objectification *on the stage*. They victoriously demonstrate the absolute preponderance of the director (*metteur en scène*) whose creative power *eliminates*

53

*words*. The themes are vague, abstract, extremely general. They are given life only by the fertility and intricacy of all the artifices of the stage which impose upon our minds like the conception of a metaphysics derived from a new use of gesture and voice.

What is in fact curious about all these gestures, these angular and abruptly abandoned attitudes, these syncopated modulations formed at the back of the throat, these musical phrases that break off short, these flights of elytra, these rustlings of branches, these sounds of hollow drums, these robot squeakings, these dances of animated manikins, is this: that through the labyrinth of their gestures, attitudes, and sudden cries, through the gyrations and turns which leave no portion of the stage space unutilized, the sense of a new physical language, based upon signs and no longer upon words, is liberated. These actors with their geometric robes seem to be animated hieroglyphs. It is not just the shape of their robes which, displacing the axis of the human figure, create beside the dress of these warriors in a state of trance and perpetual war a kind of second, symbolic dress and thus inspire an intellectual idea, or which merely connect, by all the intersections of their lines, with all the intersections of perspective in space. No, these spiritual signs have a precise meaning which strikes us only intuitively but with enough violence to make useless any translation into logical discursive language. And for the lovers of realism at all costs, who might find exhausting these perpetual allusions to secret attitudes inaccessible to thought, there remains the eminently realistic play of the double who is terrified by the apparitions from beyond. In this double—trembling, yelping childishly, these heels striking the ground in cadences that follow the very automatism of the liberated unconscious, this momentary concealment behind his own reality—*there* is a description of fear valid in every latitude, an indication that in the human as well as the superhuman the Orientals are more than a match for us in matters of reality.

The Balinese, who have a vocabulary of gesture and mime for every circumstance of life, reinstate the superior worth of theatrical conventions, demonstrate the forcefulness and greater emotional value of a certain number of perfectly learned and above all masterfully applied conventions. One of the reasons for our delight in this faultless performance lies precisely in the use these actors make of an exact quantity of specific gestures, of well-tried mime at a given point, and above all in the prevailing spiritual tone, the deep and subtle study that has presided at the elaboration of these plays of expression, these powerful signs which give us the impression that their power has not weakened during thousands of years. These mechanically rolling eyes, pouting lips, and muscular spasms, all producing methodically calculated effects which forbid any recourse to spontaneous improvisation, these horizontally moving heads that seem to glide from one shoulder to the other as if on rollers, everything that might correspond to immediate psychological necessities, corresponds as well to a sort of spiritual architecture, created out of gesture and mime but also out of the evocative power of a system, the musical quality of a physical movement, the parallel and admirably fused harmony of a tone. This may perhaps shock our European sense of stage freedom and spontaneous inspiration, but let no one say that this mathematics creates sterility or uniformity. The marvel is that a sensation of richness, of fantasy and prodigality emanates from this spectacle ruled with a maddening scrupulosity and consciousness. And the most commanding interpenetrations join sight to sound, intellect to sensibility, the gesture of a character to the evocation of a plant's movement across the scream of an instrument. The sighs of wind instruments prolong the vibrations of vocal cords with a sense of such oneness that you do not know whether it is the voice itself that is continuing or the identity which has absorbed the voice from the beginning. A rippling of joints, the musical angle made by the arm with the forearm, a foot falling, a knee bending, fingers that seem to be coming loose from the hand, it is all like a perpetual play of mirrors in which human limbs seem resonant with echoes, harmonies in which the notes of the orchestra, the whispers of wind instruments evoke the idea of a monstrous aviary in which the actors themselves would be the fluttering wings. Our theater which has never had the idea of this metaphysics of gesture nor known how to make music serve such immediate, such concrete dramatic ends, our purely verbal theater, unaware of everything that makes theater, of everything that exists in the air of the stage, which is measured and circumscribed by that air and has a density in space—movements, shapes, colors, vibrations, attitudes, screams—our theater might, with respect to the unmeasurable, which derives from the mind's capacity for receiving suggestion, be given lessons in spirituality from the Balinese theater. This purely popular and not sacred theater gives us an extraordinary idea of the intellectual level of a people who take the struggles of a soul preyed upon by ghosts and phantoms from the beyond as the basis for their civic festivals. For it is indeed a purely interior struggle that is staged in the last part of the spectacle. And we can remark in passing on the degree of theatrical sumptuousness which the Balinese have been able to give this struggle: their sense of the plastic requirements of the stage is equalled only by their knowledge of physical fear and the means of unleashing it. And there is in the truly terrifying look of their devil (probably Tibetan) a striking similarity to the look of a certain puppet in our own remembrance, a puppet with swollen hands of white gelatine and nails of green foliage, which was the most beautiful ornament of one of the first plays performed by Alfred Jarry's theater.

This spectacle is more than we can assimilate, assailing us with a superabundance of impressions, each richer than the next, but in a language to which it seems we no longer have the key; and this kind of irritation created by the impossibility of finding the thread and tracking the beast down—the impossibility of putting one's ear closer to the instrument in order to hear better—is one charm the more to the credit of this spectacle. And by language I do not mean an idiom indecipherable at first hearing, but precisely that sort of theatrical language foreign to every *spoken tongue*, a language in which an overwhelming stage experience seems to be communicated, in comparison with which our productions depending exclusively upon dialogue seem like so much stuttering.

What is in fact most striking in this spectacle—so well contrived to disconcert our Occidental conceptions of theater that many will deny it has any theatrical quality, whereas it is the most beautiful manifestation of pure theater it has been our privilege to see—what is striking and disconcerting for Europeans like ourselves is the admirable intellectuality that one senses crackling everywhere in the close and subtle web of gestures, in the infinitely varied modulations of voice, in this sonorous rain resounding as if from an immense dripping forest, and in the equally sonorous interlacing of movements. There is no transition from a gesture to a cry or a sound: all the senses interpenetrate, as if through strange channels hollowed out in the mind itself!

Here is a whole collection of ritual gestures to which we do not have the key and which seem to obey extremely precise musical indications, with something more that does not generally belong to music and seems intended to encircle thought, to hound it down and lead it into an inextricable and certain system. In fact everything in this theater is calculated with an enchanting mathematical meticulousness. Nothing is left to chance or to personal initiative. It is a kind of superior dance, in which the dancers were actors first of all.

Repeatedly they seem to accomplish a kind of recovery with measured steps. Just when they appear to be lost in the middle of an inextricable labyrinth of measures or about to overturn in the confusion, they have their own way of recovering equilibrium, a particular buttressing of the body, of the twisted legs, which gives the impression of a sopping rag being wrung out in tempo;—and on three final steps, which lead them ineluctably to the middle of the stage, the suspended rhythm is completed, the measure made clear.

Everything is thus regulated and impersonal; not a movement of the muscles, not the rolling of an eye but seem to belong to a kind of reflective mathematics which controls everything and by means of which everything happens. And the strange thing is that in this systematic depersonalization, in these purely muscular facial expressions, applied to the features like masks, everything produces a significance, everything affords the maximum effect.

A kind of terror seizes us at the thought of these mechanized beings, whose joys and griefs seem not their own but at the service of age-old rites, as if they were dictated by superior intelligences. In the last analysis it is this impression of a superior and prescribed Life which strikes us most in this spectacle that so much resembles a rite one might profane. It has the solemnity of a sacred rite—the hieratic quality of the costumes gives each actor a double body and a double set of limbs—and the dancer bundled into his costume seems to be nothing more than his own effigy. Over and beyond the music's broad, overpowering rhythm there is another extremely fragile, hesitant, and sustained music in which, it seems, the most precious metals are being pulverized, where springs of water are bubbling up as in the state of nature, and long processions of insects file through the plants, with a sound like that of light itself, in which the noises of deep solitudes seem to be distilled into showers of crystals, etc. . . .

Furthermore all these sounds are linked to movements, as if they were the natural consummation of gestures which have the same musical quality, and this with such a sense of musical analogy that the mind finally finds itself doomed to confusion, attributing to the separate gesticulations of the dancers the sonorous properties of the orchestra—and vice versa.

An impression of inhumanity, of the divine, of miraculous revelation is further provided by the exquisite beauty of the women's headdress: this series of banked luminous circles, made from combinations of multicolored feathers or from pearls of so beautiful a coloration that their combination has a quality of *revelation*, and the crests of which tremble rhythmically, responding *consciously*, or so it seems, to the tremblings of the body.—There are also the other headdresses of sacerdotal character, in the shape of tiaras and topped with egret crests and stiff flowers in pairs of contrasting, strangely harmonizing colors.

This dazzling ensemble full of explosions, flights, secret streams, detours in every direction of both external and internal perception, composes a sovereign idea of the theater, as it has been preserved for us down through the centuries in order to teach us what the theater never should have ceased to be. And this impression is doubled by the fact that this spectacle—popular, it seems, and secular—is like the common bread of artistic sensations among those people.

Setting aside the prodigious mathematics of this spectacle, what seems most surprising and astonishing to us is this aspect of *matter as revelation*, suddenly dispersed in signs to teach us the metaphysical identity of concrete and abstract and to teach us this *in gestures made to last*. For though we are familiar with the realistic aspect of matter, it is here developed to the $n^{th}$ power and definitively stylized.

.. .. .. .. .. .. .. .. .. .. ..

In this theater all creation comes from the stage, finds its expression and its origins alike in a secret psychic impulse which is Speech before words.

.. .. .. .. .. .. .. .. .. .. ..

It is a theater which eliminates the author in favor of what we would call, in our Occidental theatrical jargon, the director; but a director who has become a kind of manager of magic, a master of sacred ceremonies. And the material on which he works, the themes he brings to throbbing life are derived not from him but from the gods. They come, it seems, from elemental interconnections of Nature which a double Spirit has fostered.

What he sets in motion is the MANIFESTED.

This is a sort of primary Physics, from which Spirit has never disengaged itself.

.. .. .. .. .. .. .. .. .. .. ..

In a spectacle like that of Balinese theater there is something that has nothing to do with entertainment, the notion of useless, artificial amusement, of an evening's pastime which is the characteristic of our theater. The Balinese productions take shape at the very heart of matter, life, reality. There is in them something of the ceremonial quality of a religious rite, in the sense that they extirpate from the mind of the onlooker all idea of pretense, of cheap imitations of reality. This intricately detailed gesticulation has one goal, an immediate goal which it approaches by efficacious means, whose efficacity we are even meant to experience immediately. The thoughts it aims at, the spiritual states it seeks to create, the mystic solutions it proposes are aroused and attained without delay or circumlocution. All of which seems to be an exorcism to make our demons FLOW.

.. .. .. .. .. .. .. .. .. .. ..

There is a low hum of instinctual matters in this theater, but they are wrought to that point of transparency, intelligence, and ductility at which they seem to furnish us in physical terms some of the spirit's most secret insights.

The themes selected derive, one might say, from the stage itself. They have reached such a point of objective materialization that one cannot imagine them outside this close perspective, this confined and limited globe of performing space.

This spectacle offers us a marvelous complex of pure stage images, for the comprehension of which a whole new language seems to have been invented: the actors with their costumes constitute veritable living, moving hieroglyphs. And these three-dimensional hieroglyphs are in turn brocaded with a certain number of gestures—mysterious signs which correspond to some unknown, fabulous, and obscure reality which we here in the Occident have completely repressed.

There is something that has this character of a magic operation in this intense liberation of signs, restrained at first and then suddenly thrown into the air.

A chaotic boiling, full of recognizable particles and at moments strangely orderly, crackles in this effervescence of painted rhythms in which the many fermatas unceasingly make their entrance like a well-calculated silence.

Of this idea of pure theater, which is merely theoretical in the Occident and to which no one has ever attempted to give the least reality, the Balinese offer us a stupefying realization, suppressing all possibility of recourse to words for the elucidation of the most abstract themes—inventing a language of gesture to be developed in space, a language without meaning except in the circumstances of the stage.

The stage space is utilized in all its dimensions and, one might say, on all possible planes. For in addition to an acute sense of plastic beauty, these gestures always have as their final goal the elucidation of a spiritual state or problem.

At least that is the way they appear to us.

No point of space and at the same time no possible suggestion has been lost. And there is a philosophical sense, so to speak, of the power which nature has of suddenly hurling everything into chaos.

.. .. .. .. .. .. .. .. .. .. .. ..

One senses in the Balinese theater a state prior to language and which can choose its own: music, gestures, movements, words.

.. .. .. .. .. .. .. .. .. .. .. ..

It is certain that this aspect of pure theater, this physics of absolute gesture which is the idea itself and which transforms the mind's conceptions into events perceptible through the labyrinths and fibrous interlacings of matter, gives us a new idea of what belongs by nature to the domain of forms and manifested matter. Those who succeed in giving a mystic sense to the simple form of a robe and who, not content with placing a man's Double next to him, confer upon each man in his robes a double made of clothes—those who pierce these illusory or secondary clothes with a saber, giving them the look of huge butterflies pinned in the air, such men have an innate sense of the absolute and magical symbolism of nature much superior to ours, and set us an example which it is only too certain our own theater technicians will be powerless to profit from.

.. .. .. .. .. .. .. .. .. .. .. ..

That intellectual space, psychic interplay, and silence solidified by thought which exist between the members of a written phrase is here, in the scenic space, traced between the members, the air, and the perspectives of a certain number of shouts, colors and movements.

.. .. .. .. .. .. .. .. .. .. .. ..

In the performances of the Balinese theater the mind has the feeling that conception at first stumbled against gesture, gained its footing in the midst of a whole ferment of visual or sonorous images, thoughts as it were in a pure state. To put it briefly and more clearly, something akin to the musical state must have existed for this *mise en scène* where everything that is a conception of the mind is only a pretext, a virtuality whose double has produced this intense stage poetry, this many-hued spatial language.

.. .. .. .. .. .. .. .. .. .. .. ..

This perpetual play of mirrors passing from color to gesture and from cry to movement leads us unceasingly along roads rough and difficult for the mind, plunges us into that state of uncertainty and ineffable anguish which is the characteristic of poetry.

These strange games of flying hands, like insects in the green air of evening, communicate a sort of horrible obsession, an inexhaustible mental ratiocination, like a mind ceaselessly taking its bearings in the maze of its unconscious.

And what this theater makes palpable for us and captures in concrete signs are much less matters of feeling than of intelligence.

And it is by intellectual paths that it introduces us into the reconquest of the signs of what exists.

From this point of view the gesture of the central dancer who always touches his head at the same place, as if wishing to indicate the position and existence of some unimaginable central eye, some intellectual egg, is highly significant.

.. .. .. .. .. .. .. .. .. .. .. ..

What occurs as a highly colored reference to physical impressions of nature is taken up again on the level of sounds, and the sound itself is only the nostalgic representation of something else, a sort of magic state where sensations have become so subtle that they are a pleasure for the spirit to frequent. And even the imitative harmonies, the sound of the rattlesnake and rustlings of dried insects against each other, suggest the glade of a swarming landscape ready to hurl itself into chaos.—And these dancers dressed in dazzling clothes,

whose bodies beneath seem wrapped in swaddling-bands!
There is something umbilical, larval in their movement. And at
the same time we must remark on the hieroglyphic aspect of
their costumes, the horizontal lines of which project beyond the
body in every direction. They are like huge insects full of lines
and segments drawn to connect them with an unknown natural
perspective of which they seem nothing more than a kind of
detached geometry.

These costumes which encircle their abstract rotations when
they walk, and the strange crisscrossings of their feet!

Each of their movements traces a line in space, completes
some unknown rigorous figure in the ritual of a hermetic
formula which an unforeseen gesture of the hand completes.

And the folds of these robes, curving above the buttocks,
hold them as if suspended in air, as if pinned to the depths of
the theater, and prolong each of their leaps into a flight.

These howls, these rolling eyes, this continuous abstraction,
these noises of branches, noises of the cutting and rolling of
wood, all within the immense area of widely diffused sounds
disgorged from many sources, combine to overwhelm the
mind, to crystallize as a new and, I dare say, concrete conception of the abstract.

And it must be noted that when this abstraction, which
springs from a marvelous scenic edifice to return into thought,
encounters in its flight certain impressions from the world
of nature, it always seizes them at the point at which their
molecular combinations are beginning to break up: a gesture
narrowly divides us from chaos.

.. .. .. .. . .. .. .. .. .. .. ..

The last part of the spectacle is—in contrast to all the dirt,
brutality, and infamy chewed up by our European stages—a
delightful anachronism. And I do not know what other theater
would dare to pin down in this way *as if true to nature* the
throes of a soul at the mercy of phantasms from the Beyond.

.. .. .. .. .. .. .. .. .. .. ..

These metaphysicians of natural disorder who in dancing
restore to us every atom of sound and every fragmentary perception as if these were now about to rejoin their own generating principles, are able to wed movment and sound so
perfectly that it seems the dancers have hollow bones to make
these noises of resonant drums and woodblocks with their
hollow wooden limbs.

Here we are suddenly in deep metaphysical anguish, and
the rigid aspect of the body in trance, stiffened by the tide of
cosmic forces which besiege it, is admirably expressed by that
frenetic dance of rigidities and angles, in which one suddenly
feels the mind begin to plummet downwards.

As if waves of matter were tumbling over each other, dash-
ing their crests into the deep and flying from all sides of the
horizon to be enclosed in one minute portion of tremor and
trance—to cover over the void of fear.

. .   . .   . .   . .   . .   . .   . .   . .   . .   . .   . .   . .

There is an absolute in these constructed perspectives, a
real physical absolute which only Orientals are capable of
envisioning—it is in the loftiness and thoughtful boldness of
their goals that these conceptions differ from our European
conceptions of theater, even more than in the strange perfection of their performances.

Advocates of the division and partitioning of genres can
pretend to see mere dancers in the magnificent artists of the
Balinese theater, dancers entrusted with the representation
of unexplained, lofty Myths whose very elevation renders the
level of our modern Occidental theater unspeakably gross and
childish. The truth is that the Balinese theater suggests, and
in its productions *enacts*, themes of pure theater upon which
the stage performance confers an intense equilibrium, a wholly
materialized gravity.

. .   . .   . .   . .   . .   . .   . .   . .   . .   . .   . .   . .

Everything in this theater is immersed in a profound intoxication which restores to us the very elements of ecstasy,

and in ecstasy we discover the dry seething, the mineral friction of plants, vestiges and ruins of trees illuminated on their faces.

Bestiality and every trace of animality are reduced to their spare gesture: mutinous noises of the splitting earth, the sap of trees, animal yawns.

The dancers' feet, in kicking aside their robes, dissolve thoughts and sensations, permitting them to recover their pure state.

And always this confrontation of the head, this Cyclops' eye, the inner eye of the mind which the right hand gropes for.

The sign language of spiritual gestures which measure, prune, fix, separate, and subdivide feelings, states of the soul, metaphysical ideas.

This theater of quintessences in which things perform a strange about-face before becoming abstractions again.

·· ·· ·· ·· ·· ·· ·· ·· ·· ·· ·· ··

Their gestures fall so accurately upon this rhythm of the hollow drums, accent it, and seize it in flight with such sureness and at such climactic moments that it seems the very abyss of their hollow limbs which the music is going to scan.

·· ·· ·· ·· ·· ·· ·· ·· ·· ·· ··

And the women's stratified, lunar eyes:
Eyes of dreams which seem to absorb our own, eyes before which we ourselves appear to be *fantome*.

·· ·· ·· ·· ·· ·· ·· ·· ·· ·· ··

Utter satisfaction from these dance gestures, from these turning feet mingling with states of the soul, from these little flying hands, these dry and precise tappings.

·· ·· ·· ·· ·· ·· ·· ·· ·· ·· ··

We are watching a mental alchemy which makes a gesture of a state of mind—the dry, naked, linear gesture all our acts could have if they sought the absolute.

·· ·· ·· ·· ·· ·· ·· ·· ·· ·· ··

It happens that this mannerism, this excessively hieratic style, with its rolling alphabet, its shrieks of splitting stones, noises of branches, noises of the cutting and rolling of wood, compose a sort of animated material murmur in the air, in space, a visual as well as audible whispering. And after an instant the magic identification is made: WE KNOW IT IS WE WHO WERE SPEAKING.

Who, after the formidable battle between Arjuna and the Dragon, will dare to say that the whole of theater is not on the stage, i.e., beyond situations and words?

The dramatic and psychological situations have passed here into the very sign language of the combat, which is a function of the mystic athletic play of bodies and the so to speak undulatory use of the stage, whose enormous spiral reveals itself in one perspective after another.

The warriors enter the mental forest rocking with fear, overwhelmed by a great shudder, a voluminous magnetic whirling in which we can sense the rush of animal or mineral meteors.

It is more than a physical tempest, it is a spiritual concussion that is signified in the general trembling of their limbs and their rolling eyes. The sonorous pulsation of their bristling heads is at times excruciating—and the music sways behind them and at the same time sustains an unimaginable space into which real pebbles finally roll.

And behind the Warrior, bristling from the formidable cosmic tempest, is the Double who struts about, given up to the childishness of his schoolboy gibes, and who, roused by the repercussion of the turmoil, moves unaware in the midst of spells of which he has understood nothing.

# V. Oriental and Occidental Theater

The Balinese theater has revealed to us a physical and non-verbal idea of the theater, in which the theater is contained within the limits of everything that can happen on a stage, independently of the written text, whereas the theater as we conceive it in the Occident has declared its alliance with the text and finds itself limited by it. For the Occidental theater the Word is everything, and there is no possibility of expression without it; the theater is a branch of literature, a kind of sonorous species of language, and even if we admit a difference between the text spoken on the stage and the text read by the eyes, if we restrict theater to what happens between cues, we have still not managed to separate it from the idea of a *performed text*.

This idea of the supremacy of speech in the theater is so deeply rooted in us, and the theater seems to such a degree merely the material reflection of the text, that everything in the theater that exceeds this text, that is not kept within its limits and strictly conditioned by it, seems to us purely a matter of *mise en scène*, and quite inferior in comparison with the text.

Presented with this subordination of theater to speech, one might indeed wonder whether the theater by any chance possesses its own language, whether it is entirely fanciful to consider it as an independent and autonomous art, of the same rank as music, painting, dance, etc. . . .

One finds in any case that this language, if it exists, is necessarily identified with the *mise en scène* considered:

1. as the visual and plastic materialization of speech,

2. as the language of everything that can be said and signified upon a stage independently of speech, everything that finds its expression in space, or that can be affected or disintegrated by it.

Once we regard this language of the *mise en scène* as the pure theatrical language, we must discover whether it can attain the same internal ends as speech, whether theatrically and from the point of view of the mind it can claim the same intellectual efficacy as the spoken language. One can wonder, in other words, whether it has the power, not to define thoughts but *to cause thinking*, whether it may not entice the mind to take profound and efficacious attitudes toward it from its own point of view.

In a word, to raise the question of the intellectual efficacity of expression by means of objective forms, of the intellectual efficacity of a language which would use only shapes, or noise, or gesture, is to raise the question of the intellectual efficacy of art.

If we have come to attribute to art nothing more than the values of pleasure and relaxation and constrain it to a purely formal use of forms within the harmony of certain external relations, that in no way spoils its profound expressive value; but the spiritual infirmity of the Occident, which is the place *par excellence* where men have confused art and aestheticism, is to think that its painting would function only as painting, dance which would be merely plastic, as if in an attempt to castrate the forms of art, to sever their ties with all the mystic attitudes they might acquire in confrontation with the absolute.

One therefore understands that the theater, to the very degree that it remains confined within its own language and in correlation with it, must break with actuality. Its object is not to resolve social or psychological conflicts, to serve as battlefield for moral passions, but to express objectively certain secret truths, to bring into the light of day by means of active gestures certain aspects of truth that have been buried under forms in their encounters with Becoming.

To do that, to link the theater to the expressive possibilities of forms, to everything in the domain of gestures, noises, colors, movements, etc., is to restore it to its original direction, to reinstate it in its religious and metaphysical aspect, is to reconcile it with the universe.

But words, it will be said, have metaphysical powers; it is not forbidden to conceive of speech as well as of gestures on the universal level, and it is on that level moreover that speech acquires its major efficacy, like a dissociative force exerted upon physical appearances, and upon all states in which the mind feels stabilized and tends towards repose. And we can readily answer that this metaphysical way of considering speech is not that of the Occidental theater, which employs speech not as an active force springing out of the destruction of appearances in order to reach the mind itself, but on the contrary as a completed stage of thought which is lost at the moment of its own exteriorization.

Speech in the Occidental theater is used only to express psychological conflicts particular to man and the daily reality of his life. His conflicts are clearly accessible to spoken language, and whether they remain in the psychological sphere or leave it to enter the social sphere, the interest of the drama will still remain a moral one according to the way in which its conflicts attack and disintegrate the characters. And it will indeed always be a matter of a domain in which the verbal solutions of speech will retain their advantage. But these moral conflicts by their very nature have no absolute need of the stage to be resolved. To cause spoken language or expression by words to dominate on the stage the objective expression of gestures and of everything which affects the mind by sensuous and spatial means is to turn one's back on the physical necessities of the stage and to rebel against its possibilities.

It must be said that the domain of the theater is not psychological but plastic and physical. And it is not a question of whether the physical language of theater is capable of achieving the same psychological resolutions as the language of words, whether it is able to express feelings and passions as well as words, but whether there are not attitudes in the realm of thought and intelligence that words are incapable of grasping and that gestures and everything partaking of a spatial language attain with more precision than they.

Before giving an example of the relations between the physical world and the deepest states of mind, let me quote what I have written elsewhere:

"All true feeling is in reality untranslatable. To express it is to betray it. But to translate it is *to dissimulate it*. True expression hides what it makes manifest. It sets the mind in opposition to the real void of nature by creating in reaction a kind of fullness in thought. Or, in other terms, in relation to the manifestation-illusion of nature it creates a void in thought. All powerful feeling produces in us the idea of the void. And the lucid language which obstructs the appearance of this void also obstructs the appearance of poetry in thought. That is why an image, an allegory, a figure that masks what it would reveal have more significance for the spirit than the lucidities of speech and its analytics.

"This is why true beauty never strikes us directly. The setting sun is beautiful because of all it makes us lose."

The nightmares of Flemish painting strike us by the juxtaposition with the real world of what is only a caricature of that world; they offer the specters we encounter in our dreams. They originate in those half-dreaming states that produce clumsy, ambiguous gestures and embarrassing slips of the tongue: beside a forgotten child they place a leaping harp; near a human embryo swimming in underground waterfalls they show an army's advance against a redoubtable fortress. Beside the imaginary uncertainty the march of certitude, and beyond a yellow subterranean light the orange flash of a great autumn sun just about to set.

It is not a matter of suppressing speech in the theater but of changing its role, and especially of reducing its position, of considering it as something else than a means of conducting human characters to their external ends, since the theater is concerned only with the way feelings and passions conflict with one another, and man with man, in life.

To change the role of speech in theater is to make use of it in a concrete and spatial sense, combining it with everything in the theater that is spatial and significant in the concrete domain;—to manipulate it like a solid object, one which overturns and disturbs things, in the air first of all, then in an infinitely more mysterious and secret domain but one that admits of extension, and it will not be very difficult to identify this secret but extended domain with that of formal anarchy on the one hand but also with that of continuous formal creation on the other.

This is why the identification of the theater's purpose with every possibility of formal and extended manifestation gives rise to the idea of a certain poetry in space which itself is taken for sorcery.

In the Oriental theater of metaphysical tendency, contrasted to the Occidental theater of psychological tendency, forms assume and extend their sense and their significations on all possible levels; or, if you will, they set up vibrations not on a single level, but on every level of the mind at once.

And it is because of the multiplicity of their aspects that they can disturb and charm and continuously excite the mind. It is because the Oriental theater does not deal with the external aspects of things on a single level nor rest content with the simple obstacle or with the impact of these aspects on the senses, but instead considers the degree of mental possibility from which they issue, that it participates in the intense poetry of nature and preserves its magic relations with all the objective degrees of universal magnetism.

It is in the light of magic and sorcery that the *mise en scène* must be considered, not as the reflection of a writtten text, the mere projection of physical doubles that is derived from the written work, but as the burning projection of all the objective consequences of a gesture, word, sound, music, and their combinations. This active projection can be made only upon the stage and its consequences found in the presence of and upon the stage; and the author who uses written words only has nothing to do with the theater and must give way to specialists in its objective and animated sorcery.

One of the reasons for the asphyxiating atmosphere in which we live without possible escape or remedy—and in which we all share, even the most revolutionary among us—is our respect for what has been written, formulated, or painted, what has been given form, as if all expression were not at last exhausted, were not at a point where things must break apart if they are to start anew and begin fresh.

We must have done with this idea of masterpieces reserved for a self-styled elite and not understood by the general public; the mind has no such restricted districts as those so often used for clandestine sexual encounters.

Masterpieces of the past are good for the past: they are not good for us. We have the right to say what has been said and even what has not been said in a way that belongs to us, a way that is immediate and direct, corresponding to present modes of feeling, and understandable to everyone.

It is idiotic to reproach the masses for having no sense of the sublime, when the sublime is confused with one or another of its formal manifestations, which are moreover always defunct manifestations. And if for example a contemporary public does not understand *Oedipus Rex*, I shall make bold to say that it is the fault of *Oedipus Rex* and not of the public.

In *Oedipus Rex* there is the theme of incest and the idea that nature mocks at morality and that there are certain unspecified powers at large which we would do well to beware of, call them *destiny* or anything you choose.

There is in addition the presence of a plague epidemic which is a physical incarnation of these powers. But the whole in a manner and language that have lost all touch with the rude and epileptic rhythm of our time. Sophocles speaks grandly perhaps, but in a style that is no longer timely. His language is too refined for this age, it is as if he were speaking beside the point.

However, a public that shudders at train wrecks, that is familiar with earthquakes, plagues, revolutions, wars; that is sensitive to the disordered anguish of love, can be affected by all these grand notions and asks only to become aware of them, but on condition that it is addressed in its own language, and that its knowledge of these things does not come to it through adulterated trappings and speech that belong to extinct eras which will never live again.

Today as yesterday, the public is greedy for mystery: it asks only to become aware of the laws according to which destiny manifests itself, and to divine perhaps the secret of its apparitions.

Let us leave textual criticism to graduate students, formal criticism to esthetes, and recognize that what has been said is not still to be said; that an expression does not have the same value twice, does not live two lives; that all words, once spoken, are dead and function only at the moment when they are uttered, that a form, once it has served, cannot be used again and asks only to be replaced by another, and that the theater is the only place in the world where a gesture, once made, can never be made the same way twice.

If the public does not frequent our literary masterpieces, it is because those masterpieces are literary, that is to say, fixed; and fixed in forms that no longer respond to the needs of the time.

Far from blaming the public, we ought to blame the formal screen we interpose between ourselves and the public, and this new form of idolatry, the idolatry of fixed masterpieces which is one of the aspects of bourgeois conformism.

This conformism makes us confuse sublimity, ideas, and things with the forms they have taken in time and in our minds—in our snobbish, precious, aesthetic mentalities which the public does not understand.

How pointless in such matters to accuse the public of bad taste because it relishes insanities, so long as the public is not shown a valid spectacle; and I defy anyone to show me *here* a spectacle valid—valid in the supreme sense of the theater— since the last great romantic melodramas, i.e., since a hundred years ago.

The public, which takes the false for the true, has the sense of the true and always responds to it when it is manifested. However it is not upon the stage that the true is to be sought nowadays, but in the street; and if the crowd in the street is offered an occasion to show its human dignity, it will always do so.

If people are out of the habit of going to the theater, if we have all finally come to think of theater as an inferior art, a means of popular distraction, and to use it as an outlet for our worst instincts, it is because we have learned too well what the theater has been, namely, falsehood and illusion. It is because we have been accustomed for four hundred years, that is since the Renaissance, to a purely descriptive and narrative theater—storytelling psychology; it is because every possible ingenuity has been exerted in bringing to life on the stage plausible but detached beings, with the spectacle on one side, the public on the other—and because the public is no longer shown anything but the mirror of itself.

Shakespeare himself is responsible for this aberration and decline, this disinterested idea of the theater which wishes a theatrical performance to leave the public intact, without setting off one image that will shake the organism to its foundations and leave an ineffaceable scar.

If, in Shakespeare, a man is sometimes preoccupied with what transcends him, it is always in order to determine the ultimate consequences of this preoccupation within him, i.e., psychology.

Psychology, which works relentlessly to reduce the unknown to the known, to the quotidian and the ordinary, is the cause of the theater's abasement and its fearful loss of energy, which seems to me to have reached its lowest point. And I think both the theater and we ourselves have had enough of psychology.

I believe furthermore that we can all agree on this matter sufficiently so that there is no need to descend to the repugnant level of the modern and French theater to condemn the theater of psychology.

Stories about money, worry over money, social careerism, the pangs of love unspoiled by altruism, sexuality sugarcoated with an eroticism that has lost its mystery have nothing to do with the theater, even if they do belong to psychology. These torments, seductions, and lusts before which we are nothing but Peeping Toms gratifying our cravings, tend to go bad, and their rot turns to revolution: we must take this into account.

But this is not our most serious concern.

If Shakespeare and his imitators have gradually insinuated the idea of art for art's sake, with art on one side and life on the other, we can rest on this feeble and lazy idea only as long as the life outside endures. But there are too many signs that everything that used to sustain our lives no longer does so, that we are all mad, desperate, and sick. And I call for *us* to react.

This idea of a detached art, of poetry as a charm which exists only to distract our leisure, is a decadent idea and an unmistakable symptom of our power to castrate.

Our literary admiration for Rimbaud, Jarry, Lautréamont, and a few others, which has driven two men to suicide, but turned into café gossip for the rest, belongs to this idea of literary poetry, of detached art, of neutral spiritual activity which creates nothing and produces nothing; and I can bear witness that at the very moment when that kind of personal poetry which involves only the man who creates it and only at the moment he creates it broke out in its most abusive fashion, the theater was scorned more than ever before by poets who have never had the sense of direct and concerted action, nor of efficacity, nor of danger.

We must get rid of our superstitious valuation of texts and *written* poetry. Written poetry is worth reading once, and then should be destroyed. Let the dead poets make way for others. Then we might even come to see that it is our veneration for what has already been created, however beautiful and valid it may be, that petrifies us, deadens our responses, and prevents us from making contact with that underlying power, call it thought-energy, the life force, the determinism of change, lunar menses, or anything you like. Beneath the poetry of the texts, there is the actual poetry, without form and without text. And just as the efficacity of masks in the magic practices of certain tribes is exhausted—and these masks are no longer good for anything except museums—so the poetic efficacity of a text is exhausted; yet the poetry and the efficacity of the theater are exhausted least quickly of all, since they permit the *action* of what is gesticulated and pronounced, and which is never made the same way twice.

It is a question of knowing what we want. If we are prepared for war, plague, famine, and slaughter we do not even need to say so, we have only to continue as we are; continue behaving like snobs, rushing en masse to hear such and such a singer, to see such and such an admirable performance which never transcends the realm of art (and even the Russian ballet at the height of its splendor never transcended the realm of art), to marvel at such and such an exhibition of painting in which exciting shapes explode here and there but at random and without any genuine consciousness of the forces they could rouse.

This empiricism, randomness, individualism, and anarchy must cease.

Enough of personal poems, benefitting those who create them much more than those who read them.

Once and for all, enough of this closed, egoistic, and personal art.

Our spiritual anarchy and intellectual disorder is a function of the anarchy of everything else—or rather, everything else is a function of this anarchy.

I am not one of those who believe that civilization has to change in order for the theater to change; but I do believe that the theater, utilized in the highest and most difficult sense possible, has the power to influence the aspect and formation of things: and the encounter upon the stage of two passionate manifestations, two living centers, two nervous magnetisms is something as entire, true, even decisive, as, in life, the encounter of one epidermis with another in a timeless debauchery.

That is why I propose a theater of cruelty.—With this mania we all have for depreciating everything, as soon as I have said "cruelty," everybody will at once take it to mean "blood." But *"theater of cruelty"* means a theater difficult and cruel for myself first of all. And, on the level of performance, it is not the cruelty we can exercise upon each other by hacking at each other's bodies, carving up our personal anatomies, or, like Assyrian emperors, sending parcels of human ears, noses, or neatly detached nostrils through the mail, but the much more terrible and necessary cruelty which things can exercise against us. We are not free. And the sky can still fall on our heads. And the theater has been created to teach us that first of all.

Either we will be capable of returning by present-day means to this superior idea of poetry and poetry-through-theater which underlies the Myths told by the great ancient tragedians, capable once more of entertaining a religious idea of the theater (without meditation, useless contemplation, and vague dreams), capable of attaining awareness and a possession of certain dominant forces, of certain notions that control all others, and (since ideas, when they are effective, carry their energy with them) capable of recovering within ourselves those energies which ultimately create order and increase the value of life, or else we might as well abandon ourselves now, without protest, and recognize that we are no longer good for anything but disorder, famine, blood, war, and epidemics.

Either we restore all the arts to a central attitude and necessity, finding an analogy between a gesture made in painting or the theater, and a gesture made by lava in a volcanic explosion, or we must stop painting, babbling, writing, or doing whatever it is we do.

I propose to bring back into the theater this elementary magical idea, taken up by modern psychoanalysis, which consists in effecting a patient's cure by making him assume the apparent and exterior attitudes of the desired condition.

I propose to renounce our empiricism of imagery, in which the unconscious furnishes images at random, and which the poet arranges at random too, calling them poetic and hence hermetic images, as if the kind of trance that poetry provides did not have its reverberations throughout the whole sensibility, in every nerve, and as if poetry were some vague force whose movements were invariable.

I propose to return through the theater to an idea of the physical knowledge of images and the means of inducing trances, as in Chinese medicine which knows, over the entire extent of the human anatomy, at what points to puncture in order to regulate the subtlest functions.

Those who have forgotten the communicative power and magical mimesis of a gesture, the theater can reinstruct, because a gesture carries its energy with it, and there are still human beings in the theater to manifest the force of the gesture made.

To create art is to deprive a gesture of its reverberation in the organism, whereas this reverberation, if the gesture is made in the conditions and with the force required, incites the organism and, through it, the entire individuality, to take attitudes in harmony with the gesture.

The theater is the only place in the world, the last general means we still possess of directly affecting the organism and, in periods of neurosis and petty sensuality like the one in which we are immersed, of attacking this sensuality by physical means it cannot withstand.

If music affects snakes, it is not on account of the spiritual notions it offers them, but because snakes are long and coil their length upon the earth, because their bodies touch the earth at almost every point; and because the musical vibrations which are communicated to the earth affect them like a very subtle, very long massage; and I propose to treat the spectators like the snakecharmer's subjects and conduct them *by means of their organisms* to an apprehension of the subtlest notions.

At first by crude means, which will gradually be refined. These immediate crude means will hold their attention at the start.

That is why in the "theater of cruelty" the spectator is in the center and the spectacle surrounds him.

In this spectacle the sonorisation is constant: sounds, noises, cries are chosen first for their vibratory quality, then for what they represent.

Among these gradually refined means light is interposed in its turn. Light which is not created merely to add color or to brighten, and which brings its power, influence, suggestions with it. And the light of a green cavern does not sensually dispose the organism like the light of a windy day.

After sound and light there is action, and the dynamism of action: here the theater, far from copying life, puts itself whenever possible in communication with pure forces. And whether you accept or deny them, there is nevertheless a way of speaking which gives the name of "forces" to whatever brings to birth images of energy in the unconscious, and gratuitous crime on the surface.

A violent and concentrated action is a kind of lyricism: it summons up supernatural images, a bloodstream of images, a bleeding spurt of images in the poet's head and in the spectator's as well.

Whatever the conflicts that haunt the mind of a given period, I defy any spectator to whom such violent scenes will have transferred their blood, who will have felt in himself the transit of a superior action, who will have seen the extraordinary and essential movements of his thought illuminated in extraordinary deeds—the violence and blood having been placed at the service of the violence of the thought—I defy that spectator to give himself up, once outside the theater, to ideas of war, riot, and blatant murder.

So expressed, this idea seems dangerous and sophomoric. It will be claimed that example breeds example, that if the attitude of cure induces cure, the attitude of murder will induce murder. Everything depends upon the manner and the purity with which the thing is done. There is a risk. But let it not be forgotten that though a theatrical gesture is violent, it is disinterested; and that the theater teaches precisely the uselessness of the action which, once done, is not to be done, and the superior use of the state unused by the action and which, *restored,* produces a purification.

I propose then a theater in which violent physical images

crush and hypnotize the sensibility of the spectator seized by the theater as by a whirlwind of higher forces.

A theater which, abandoning psychology, recounts the extraordinary, stages natural conflicts, natural and subtle forces, and presents itself first of all as an exceptional power of redirection. A theater that induces trance, as the dances of Dervishes induce trance, and that addresses itself to the organism by precise instruments, by the same means as those of certain tribal music cures which we admire on records but are incapable of originating among ourselves.

There is a risk involved, but in the present circumstances I believe it is a risk worth running. I do not believe we have managed to revitalize the world we live in, and I do not believe it is worth the trouble of clinging to; but I do propose something to get us out of our marasmus, instead of continuing to complain about it, and about the boredom, inertia, and stupidity of everything.

## VII. The Theater and Cruelty

An idea of the theater has been lost. And as long as the theater limits itself to showing us intimate scenes from the lives of a few puppets, transforming the public into Peeping Toms, it is no wonder the elite abandon it and the great public looks to the movies, the music hall or the circus for violent satisfactions, whose intentions do not deceive them.

( At the point of deterioration which our sensibility has reached, it is certain that we need above all a theater that wakes us up: nerves and heart. )

The misdeeds of the psychological theater descended from Racine have unaccustomed us to that immediate and violent action which the theater should possess. Movies in their turn, murdering us with second-hand reproductions which, filtered through machines, cannot *unite with* our sensibility, have maintained us for ten years in an ineffectual torpor, in which all our faculties appear to be foundering.

In the anguished, catastrophic period we live in, we feel an urgent need for a theater which events do not exceed, whose resonance is deep within us, dominating the instability of the times.

( Our long habit of seeking diversion has made us forget the idea of a serious theater, which, overturning all our preconceptions, inspires us with the fiery magnetism of its images and acts upon us like a spiritual therapeutics whose touch can never be forgotten.)

Everything that acts is a cruelty. It is upon this idea of extreme action, pushed beyond all limits, that theater must be rebuilt.

Imbued with the idea that the public thinks first of all with its senses and that to address oneself first to its understanding as the ordinary psychological theater does is absurd, the Theater of Cruelty proposes to resort to a mass spectacle; to seek in the agitation of tremendous masses, convulsed and hurled against each other, a little of that poetry of festivals and crowds when, all too rarely nowadays, the people pour out into the streets.

The theater must give us everything that is in crime, love, war, or madness, if it wants to recover its necessity.

Everyday love, personal ambition, struggles for status, all have value only in proportion to their relation to the terrible lyricism of the Myths to which the great mass of men have assented.

This is why we shall try to concentrate, around famous personages, atrocious crimes, superhuman devotions, a drama which, without resorting to the defunct images of the old Myths, shows that it can extract the forces which struggle within them.

In a word, we believe that there are living forces in what is called poetry and that the image of a crime presented in the requisite theatrical conditions is something infinitely more terrible for the spirit than that same crime when actually committed.

We want to make out of the theater a believable reality which gives the heart and the senses that kind of concrete bite which all true sensation requires. In the same way that our dreams have an effect upon us and reality has an effect upon our dreams, so we believe that the images of thought can be identified with a dream which will be efficacious to the degree that it can be projected with the necessary violence. And the public will believe in the theater's dreams on condition that it take them for true dreams and not for a servile copy of reality; on condition that they allow the public to liberate within itself the magical liberties of dreams which it can only recognize when they are imprinted with terror and cruelty.

Hence this appeal to cruelty and terror, though on a vast scale, whose range probes our entire vitality, confronts us with all our possibilities.

It is in order to attack the spectator's sensibility on all sides that we advocate a revolving spectacle which, instead of making the stage and auditorium two closed worlds, without possible communication, spreads its visual and sonorous outbursts over the entire mass of the spectators.

Also, departing from the sphere of analyzable passions, we intend to make use of the actor's lyric qualities to manifest external forces, and by this means to cause the whole of nature to re-enter the theater in its restored form.

However vast this program may be, it does not exceed the theater itself, which appears to us, all in all, to identify itself with the forces of ancient magic.

Practically speaking, we want to resuscitate an idea of total spectacle by which the theater would recover from the cinema, the music hall, the circus, and from life itself what has always belonged to it. The separation between the analytic theater and the plastic world seems to us a stupidity. One does not separate the mind from the body nor the senses from the intelligence, especially in a domain where the endlessly renewed fatigue of the organs requires intense and sudden shocks to revive our understanding.

Thus, on the one hand, the mass and extent of a spectacle

addressed to the entire organism; on the other, an intensive mobilization of objects, gestures, and signs, used in a new spirit. The reduced role given to the understanding leads to an energetic compression of the text; the active role given to obscure poetic emotion necessitates concrete signs. Words say little to the mind; extent and objects speak; new images speak, even new images made with words. But space thundering with images and crammed with sounds speaks too, if one knows how to intersperse from time to time a sufficient extent of space stocked with silence and immobility.

On this principle we envisage producing a spectacle where these means of direct action are used in their totality; a spectacle unafraid of going as far as necessary in the exploration of our nervous sensibility, of which the rhythms, sounds, words, resonances, and twitterings, and their united quality and surprising mixtures belong to a technique which must not be divulged.

The images in certain paintings by Grunewald or Hieronymus Bosch tell enough about what a spectacle can be in which, as in the brain of some saint, the objects of external nature will appear as temptations.

It is in this spectacle of a temptation from which life has everything to lose and the mind everything to gain that the theater must recover its true signification.

Elsewhere we have given a program which will allow the means of pure staging, found on the spot, to be organized around historic or cosmic themes, familiar to all.

And we insist on the fact that the first spectacle of the Theater of Cruelty will turn upon the preoccupations of the great mass of men, preoccupations much more pressing and disquieting than those of any individual whatsoever.

It is a matter of knowing whether now, in Paris, before the cataclysms which are at our door descend upon us, sufficient means of production, financial or otherwise, can be found to permit such a theater to be brought to life—it is bound to in any case, because it is the future. Or whether a little real blood will be needed, right away, in order to manifest this cruelty.

*May 1933.*

# VIII. The Theater of Cruelty (First Manifesto)

We cannot go on prostituting the idea of theater whose only value is in its excruciating, magical relation to reality and danger.

Put in this way, the question of the theater ought to arouse general attention, the implication being that theater, through its physical aspect, since it requires *expression in space* (the only real expression, in fact), allows the magical means of art and speech to be exercised organically and altogether, like renewed exorcisms. The upshot of all this is that theater will not be given its specific powers of action until it is given its language.

That is to say: instead of continuing to rely upon texts considered definitive and sacred, it is essential to put an end to the subjugation of the theater to the text, and to recover the notion of a kind of unique language half-way between gesture and thought.

This language cannot be defined except by its possibilities for dynamic expression in space as opposed to the expressive possibilities of spoken dialogue. And what the theater can still take over from speech are its possibilities for extension beyond words, for development in space, for dissociative and vibratory action upon the sensibility. This is the hour of intonations, of a word's particular pronunciation. Here too intervenes (besides the auditory language of sounds) the visual language of objects, movements, attitudes, and gestures, but on condition that their meanings, their physiognomies, their combinations be carried to the point of becoming signs, making a kind of alphabet out of these signs. Once aware of this language in space, language of sounds, cries, lights, onomatopoeia, the theater must organize it into veritable hieroglyphs, with the help of characters and objects, and make use of their symbolism and interconnections in relation to all organs and on all levels.

The question, then, for the theater, is to create a metaphysics of speech, gesture, and expression, in order to rescue it from its servitude to psychology and "human interest." But all this can be of no use unless behind such an effort there is some kind of real metaphysical inclination, an appeal to certain unhabitual ideas, which by their very nature cannot be limited or even formally depicted. These ideas which touch on Creation, Becoming, and Chaos, are all of a cosmic order and furnish a primary notion of a domain from which the theater is now entirely alien. They are able to create a kind of passionate equation between Man, Society, Nature, and Objects.

It is not, moreover, a question of bringing metaphysical ideas directly onto the stage, but of creating what you might call temptations, indraughts of air around these ideas. And humor with its anarchy, poetry with its symbolism and its images, furnish a basic notion of ways to channel the temptation of these ideas.

We must speak now about the uniquely material side of this language—that is, about all the ways and means it has of acting upon the sensibility.

It would be meaningless to say that it includes music, dance, pantomime, or mimicry. Obviously it uses movement,

harmonies, rhythms, but only to the point that they can con-
cur in a sort of central expression without advantage for any
one particular art. This does not at all mean that it does not
use ordinary actions, ordinary passions, but like a springboard uses them in the same way that HUMOR AS DESTRUC-
TION can serve to reconcile the corrosive nature of laughter
to the habits of reason.

But by an altogether Oriental means of expression, this
objective and concrete language of the theater can fascinate
and ensnare the organs. It flows into the sensibility. Abandoning Occidental usages of speech, it turns words into incantations. It extends the voice. It utilizes the vibrations and
qualities of the voice. It wildly tramples rhythms underfoot.
It pile-drives sounds. It seeks to exalt, to benumb, to charm,
to arrest the sensibility. It liberates a new lyricism of gesture
which, by its precipitation or its amplitude in the air, ends by
surpassing the lyricism of words. It ultimately breaks away
from the intellectual subjugation of the language, by convey-
ing the sense of a new and deeper intellectuality which hides
itself beneath the gestures and signs, raised to the dignity of
particular exorcisms.

For all this magnetism, all this poetry, and all these direct
means of spellbinding would be nothing if they were not used
to put the spirit physically on the track of something else,
if the true theater could not give us the sense of a creation
of which we possess only one face, but which is completed
on other levels.

And it is of little importance whether these other levels
are really conquered by the mind or not, i.e., by the intelligence; it would diminish them, and that has neither interest
nor sense. What is important is that, by positive means, the
sensitivity is put in a state of deepened and keener perception,
and this is the very object of the magic and the rites of which
the theater is only a reflection.

### TECHNIQUE

It is a question then of making the theater, in the proper sense of the word, a function; something as localized and as precise as the circulation of the blood in the arteries or the apparently chaotic development of dream images in the brain, and this is to be accomplished by a thorough involvement, a genuine enslavement of the attention.

The theater will never find itself again—i.e., constitute a means of true illusion—except by furnishing the spectator with the truthful precipitates of dreams, in which his taste for crime, his erotic obsessions, his savagery, his chimeras, his utopian sense of life and matter, even his cannibalism, pour out, on a level not counterfeit and illusory, but interior.

In other terms, the theater must pursue by all its means a reassertion not only of all the aspects of the objective and descriptive external world, but of the internal world, that is, of man considered metaphysically. It is only thus, we believe, that we shall be able to speak again in the theater about the rights of the imagination. Neither humor, nor poetry, nor imagination means anything unless, by an anarchistic destruction generating a prodigious flight of forms which will constitute the whole spectacle, they succeed in organically re-involving man, his ideas about reality, and his poetic place in reality.

To consider the theater as a second-hand psychological or moral function, and to believe that dreams themselves have only a substitute function, is to diminish the profound poetic bearing of dreams as well as of the theater. If the theater, like dreams, is bloody and inhuman, it is, more than just that, to manifest and unforgettably root within us the idea of a perpetual conflict, a spasm in which life is continually lacerated, in which everything in creation rises up and exerts itself against our appointed rank; it is in order to perpetuate in a concrete and immediate way the metaphysical ideas of certain

Fables whose very atrocity and energy suffice to show their origin and continuity in essential principles.

This being so, one sees that, by its proximity to principles which transfer their energy to it poetically, this naked language of the theater (not a virtual but a real language) must permit, by its use of man's nervous magnetism, the transgression of the ordinary limits of art and speech, in order to realize actively, that is to say magically, *in real terms,* a kind of total creation in which man must reassume his place between dream and events.

### THE THEMES

It is not a matter of boring the public to death with transcendent cosmic preoccupations. That there may be profound keys to thought and action with which to interpret the whole spectacle, does not in general concern the spectator, who is simply not interested. But still they must be there; and that concerns us.

THE SPECTACLE: *Every spectacle will contain a physical and objective element, perceptible to all. Cries, groans, apparitions, surprises, theatricalities of all kinds, magic beauty of costumes taken from certain ritual models; resplendent lighting, incantational beauty of voices, the charms of harmony, rare notes of music, colors of objects, physical rhythm of movements whose crescendo and decrescendo will accord exactly with the pulsation of movements familiar to everyone, concrete appearances of new and surprising objects, masks, effigies yards high, sudden changes of light, the physical action of light which arouses sensations of heat and cold, etc.*

THE MISE EN SCENE: *The typical language of the theater will be constituted around the* mise en scène *considered not simply as the degree of refraction of a text upon the stage, but as the point of departure for all theatrical creation. And it is in the use and handling of this language that the old duality between author and director will be dissolved, replaced by a sort of unique Creator upon whom will devolve the double responsibility of the spectacle and the plot.*

THE LANGUAGE OF THE STAGE: *It is not a question of suppressing the spoken language, but of giving words approximately the importance they have in dreams.*

*Meanwhile new means of recording this language must be found, whether these means belong to musical transcription or to some kind of code.*

*As for ordinary objects, or even the human body, raised to the dignity of signs, it is evident that one can draw one's inspiration from hieroglyphic characters, not only in order to record these signs in a readable fashion which permits them to be reproduced at will, but in order to compose on the stage precise and immediately readable symbols.*

*On the other hand, this code language and musical transcription will be valuable as a means of transcribing voices.*

*Since it is fundamental to this language to make a particular use of intonations, these intonations will constitute a kind of harmonic balance, a secondary deformation of speech which must be reproducible at will.*

*Similarly the ten thousand and one expressions of the face caught in the form of masks can be labeled and catalogued, so they may eventually participate directly and symbolically in this concrete language of the stage, independently of their particular psychological use.*

*Moreover, these symbolical gestures, masks, and attitudes, these individual or group movements whose innumerable meanings constitute an important part of the concrete language of the theater, evocative gestures, emotive or arbitrary attitudes, excited pounding out of rhythms and sounds, will be doubled, will be multiplied by reflections, as it were, of the gestures and attitudes consisting of the mass of all the impulsive gestures, all the abortive attitudes, all the lapses of mind and tongue, by which are revealed what might be called the impotences of speech, and in which is a prodigious wealth of expressions, to which we shall not fail to have recourse on occasion.*

*There is, besides, a concrete idea of music in which the sounds make their entrance like characters, where harmonies are coupled together and lose themselves in the precise entrances of words.*

*From one means of expression to another, correspondences and levels of development are created—even light can have a precise intellectual meaning.*

MUSICAL INSTRUMENTS: *They will be treated as objects and as part of the set.*

*Also, the need to act directly and profoundly upon the sensibility through the organs invites research, from the point of view of sound, into qualities and vibrations of absolutely new sounds, qualities which present-day musical instruments do not possess and which require the revival of ancient and forgotten instruments or the invention of new ones. Research is also required, apart from music, into instruments and appliances which, based upon special combinations or new alloys of metal, can attain a new range and compass, producing sounds or noises that are unbearably piercing.*

LIGHTS, LIGHTING: *The lighting equipment now in use in theaters is no longer adequate. The particular action of light upon the mind, the effects of all kinds of luminous vibration must be investigated, along with new ways of spreading the light in waves, in sheets, in fusillades of fiery arrows. The color gamut of the equipment now in use is to be revised from beginning to end. In order to produce the qualities of particular musical tones, light must recover an element of thinness, density, and opaqueness, with a view to producing the sensations of heat, cold, anger, fear, etc.*

COSTUMES: *Where costumes are concerned, modern dress will be avoided as much as possible without at the same time assuming a uniform theatrical costuming that would be the same for every play—not from a fetishist and superstitious reverence for the past, but because it seems absolutely evident that certain age-old costumes, of ritual intent, though they existed at a given moment of time, preserve a beauty and a revelational appearance from their closeness to the traditions that gave them birth.*

THE STAGE—THE AUDITORIUM: *We abolish the stage and the auditorium and replace them by a single site, without partition or barrier of any kind, which will become the theater of the action. A direct communication will be re-established between the spectator and the spectacle, between the actor and the spectator, from the fact that the spectator, placed in the middle of the action, is engulfed and physically affected by it. This envelopment results, in part, from the very configuration of the room itself.*

*Thus, abandoning the architecture of present-day theaters, we shall take some hangar or barn, which we shall have reconstructed according to processes which have culminated in the architecture of certain churches or holy places, and of certain temples in Tibet.*

*In the interior of this construction special proportions of height and depth will prevail. The hall will be enclosed by four walls, without any kind of ornament, and the public will be seated in the middle of the room, on the ground floor, on mobile chairs which will allow them to follow the spectacle which will take place all around them. In effect, the absence of a stage in the usual sense of the word will provide for the deployment of the action in the four corners of the room. Particular positions will be reserved for actors and action at the four cardinal points of the room. The scenes will be played in front of whitewashed wall-backgrounds designed to absorb the light. In addition, galleries overhead will run around the periphery of the hall as in certain primitive paintings. These galleries will permit the actors, whenever the action makes it necessary, to be pursued from one point in the room to another, and the action to be deployed on all levels and in all perspectives of height and depth. A cry uttered at one end of the room can be transmitted from mouth to mouth with amplifications and successive modulations all the way to the other. The action will unfold, will extend its trajectory from level to level, point to point; paroxysms will suddenly burst forth, will flare up like fires in different spots. And to speak of the spectacle's character as true illusion or of the direct and immediate influence of the action on the spectator will not be hollow words. For this diffusion of action over an immense space will oblige the lighting of a scene and the varied lighting of a performance to fall upon the public as much as upon the actors—and to the several simultaneous actions or several phases of an identical action in which the characters, swarming over each other like bees, will endure all the onslaughts of the situations and the external assaults of the tempestuous elements, will correspond the physical means of lighting, of producing thunder or wind, whose repercussions the spectator will undergo.*

*However, a central position will be reserved which, without serving, properly speaking, as a stage, will permit the bulk of the action to be concentrated and brought to a climax whenever necessary.*

OBJECTS—MASKS—ACCESSORIES: *Manikins, enormous masks, objects of strange proportions will appear with the same sanction as verbal images, will enforce the concrete aspect of every image and every expression—with the corollary that all objects requiring a stereotyped physical representation will be discarded or disguised.*

THE SET: *There will not be any set. This function will be sufficiently undertaken by hieroglyphic characters, ritual costumes, manikins ten feet high representing the beard of King*

*Lear in the storm, musical instruments tall as men, objects of unknown shape and purpose.*

IMMEDIACY: *But, people will say, a theater so divorced from life, from facts, from immediate interests. . . . From the present and its events, yes! From whatever preoccupations have any of that profundity which is the prerogative of some men, no! In the* Zohar, *the story of Rabbi Simeon who burns like fire is as immediate as fire itself.*

WORKS: *We shall not act a written play, but we shall make attempts at direct staging, around themes, facts, or known works. The very nature and disposition of the room suggest this treatment, and there is no theme, however vast, that can be denied us.*

SPECTACLE: *There is an idea of integral spectacles which must be regenerated. The problem is to make space speak, to feed and furnish it; like mines laid in a wall of rock which all of a sudden turns into geysers and bouquets of stone.*

THE ACTOR: *The actor is both an element of first importance, since it is upon the effectiveness of his work that the success of the spectacle depends, and a kind of passive and neutral element, since he is rigorously denied all personal initiative. It is a domain in which there is no precise rule; and between the actor of whom is required the mere quality of a sob and the actor who must deliver an oration with all his personal qualities of persuasiveness, there is the whole margin which separates a man from an instrument.*

THE INTERPRETATION: *The spectacle will be calculated from one end to the other, like a code* (un langage). *Thus there will be no lost movements, all movements will obey a rhythm; and each character being merely a type, his gesticulation, physiognomy, and costume will appear like so many rays of light.*

THE CINEMA: *To the crude visualization of what is, the theater through poetry opposes images of what is not. However, from the point of view of action, one cannot compare a cinematic image which, however poetic it may be, is limited by the film, to a theatrical image which obeys all the exigencies of life.*

CRUELTY: *Without an element of cruelty at the root of every spectacle, the theater is not possible. In our present state of degeneration it is through the skin that metaphysics must be made to re-enter our minds.*

THE PUBLIC: *First of all this theater must exist.*

THE PROGRAM: *We shall stage, without regard for text:*

*1. An adaptation of a work from the time of Shakespeare, a work entirely consistent with our present troubled state of mind, whether one of the apocryphal plays of Shakespeare, such as* Arden of Feversham, *or an entirely different play from the same period.*

*2. A play of extreme poetic freedom by Leon-Paul Fargue.*

*3. An extract from the* Zohar: *The Story of Rabbi Simeon, which has the ever present violence and force of a conflagration.*

*4. The story of Bluebeard reconstructed according to the historical records and with a new idea of eroticism and cruelty.*

*5. The Fall of Jerusalem, according to the Bible and history; with the blood-red color that trickles from it and the people's feeling of abandon and panic visible even in the light; and on the other hand the metaphysical disputes of the prophets, the frightful intellectual agitation they create and the repercussions of which physically affect the King, the Temple, the People, and Events themselves.*

*6. A Tale by the Marquis de Sade, in which the eroticism will be transposed, allegorically mounted and figured, to create a violent exteriorization of cruelty, and a dissimulation of the remainder.*

*7. One or more romantic melodramas in which the improbability will become an active and concrete element of poetry.*

*8. Büchner's* Wozzek, *in a spirit of reaction against our principles and as an example of what can be drawn from a formal text in terms of the stage.*

*9. Works from the Elizabethan theater stripped of their text and retaining only the accouterments of period, situations, characters, and action.*

## IX. Letters on Cruelty

*To J. P.*                    *Paris, September 13, 1932*

Dear friend,

I cannot give you particulars about my Manifesto that would risk emasculating its point. All I can do is to comment, for the time being, upon my title "Theater of Cruelty" and try to justify its choice.

This Cruelty is a matter of neither sadism nor bloodshed, at least not in any exclusive way.

I do not systematically cultivate horror. The word "cruelty" must be taken in a broad sense, and not in the rapacious physical sense that it is customarily given. And I claim, in doing this, the right to break with the usual sense of language, to crack the armature once and for all, to get the iron collar off its neck, in short to return to the etymological origins of speech which, in the midst of abstract concepts, always evoke a concrete element.

One can very well imagine a pure cruelty, without bodily laceration. And philosophically speaking what indeed is cruelty? From the point of view of the mind, cruelty signifies rigor, implacable intention and decision, irreversible and absolute determination.

The most current philosophical determinism is, from the point of view of our existence, an image of cruelty.

It is a mistake to give the word 'cruelty' a meaning of merciless bloodshed and disinterested, gratuitous pursuit of physical suffering. The Ethiopian Ras who carts off vanquished princes and makes them his slaves does not do so out of a desperate love of blood. Cruelty is not synonymous with bloodshed, martyred flesh, crucified enemies. This identification of cruelty with tortured victims is a very minor aspect of the question. In the practice of cruelty there is a kind of higher determinism, to which the executioner-tormenter himself is subjected and which he must be *determined* to endure when the time comes. Cruelty is above all lucid, a kind of rigid control and submission to necessity. There is no cruelty without consciousness and without the application of consciousness. It is consciousness that gives to the exercise of every act of life its blood-red color, its cruel nuance, since it is understood that life is always someone's death.

### SECOND LETTER

*To J. P.*                                        *Paris, November 14, 1932*

Dear friend,

Cruelty was not tacked onto my thinking; it has always been at home there: but I had to become conscious of it. I employ the word 'cruelty' in the sense of an appetite for life, a cosmic rigor and implacable necessity, in the gnostic sense of a living whirlwind that devours the darkness, in the sense of that pain apart from whose ineluctable necessity life could not continue; good is desired, it is the consequence of an act; evil is permanent. When the hidden god creates, he obeys the cruel necessity of creation which has been imposed on himself by himself, and he cannot *not* create, hence not admit into the center of the self-willed whirlwind a kernel of evil ever more condensed, and ever more consumed. And theater in the sense of continuous creation, a wholly magical action, obeys this necessity. A play in which there would not be this will, this blind appetite for life capable of overriding everything, visible in each gesture and each act and in the transcendent aspect of the story, would be a useless and unfulfilled play.

### THIRD LETTER

*To M. R. de R.*                          *Paris, November 16, 1932*

Dear friend,

I confess to you I neither understand nor admit the objections that have been made against my title. For it seems to me that creation and life itself are defined only by a kind of rigor, hence a fundamental cruelty, which leads things to their ineluctable end at whatever cost.

Effort is a cruelty, existence through effort is a cruelty. Rising from his repose and extending himself into being, Brahma suffers, with a suffering that yields joyous harmonics perhaps, but which at the ultimate extremity of the curve can only be expressed by a terrible crushing and grinding.

There is in life's flame, life's appetite, life's irrational impulsion, a kind of initial perversity: the desire characteristic of Eros is cruelty since it feeds upon contingencies; death is cruelty, resurrection is cruelty, transfiguration is cruelty, since nowhere in a circular and closed world is there room for true death, since ascension is a rending, since closed space is fed with lives, and each stronger life tramples down the others, consuming them in a massacre which is a transfiguration and a bliss. In the manifested world, metaphysically speaking, evil is the permanent law, and what is good is an effort and already one more cruelty added to the other.

Not to understand this is not to understand metaphysical ideas. And after this let no one come to tell me my title is too limited. It is cruelty that cements matter together, cruelty that molds the features of the created world. Good is always upon the outer face, but the face within is evil. Evil which will eventually be reduced, but at the supreme instant when everything that was form will be on the point of returning to chaos.

# X. Letters on Language

*To M. B. C.*                    *Paris, September 15, 1931*

Sir,

You state in an article on the theater and the *mise en scène* that "in considering the *mise en scène* as an autonomous art one risks committing still worse errors" and that "the presentation, the spectacular aspect of a dramatic work should not be determined in total and cavalier independence."

And you say in addition that these are elementary truths.

You are perfectly right in considering the *mise en scène* as only a subservient and minor art to which even those who employ it with the maximum of independence deny all fundamental originality. So long as the *mise en scène* remains, even in the minds of the boldest directors, a simple means of presentation, an accessory mode of expressing the work, a sort of spectacular intermediary with no significance of its own, it will be valuable only to the degree it succeeds in hiding itself behind the works it is pretending to serve. And this will continue as long as the major interest in a performed work is in its text, as long as literature takes precedence over the kind of performance improperly called spectacle, with everything pejorative, accessory, ephemeral, and external that that term carries with it.

Here is what seems to me an elementary truth that must precede any other: namely, that the theater, an independent and autonomous art, must, in order to revive or simply to live, realize what differentiates it from text, pure speech, literature, and all other fixed and written means.

We can perfectly well continue to conceive of a theater based upon the authority of the text, and on a text more and more wordy, diffuse, and boring, to which the esthetics of the stage would be subject.

But this conception of theater, which consists of having people sit on a certain number of straight-backed or over-stuffed chairs placed in a row and tell each other stories, however marvelous, is, if not the absolute negation of theater —which does not absolutely require movement in order to be what it should—certainly its perversion.

For the theater to become an essentially psychological matter, the intellectual alchemy of feelings, and for the pin-nacle of art in the dramatic medium to consist finally in a certain ideal of silence and immobility, is nothing but the perversion on the stage of the idea of concentration.

This concentration in playing, employed among so many modes of expression by the Japanese for example, is valuable as only one means among many others. And to make a goal out of it on the stage is to abstain from making use of the stage, like someone who, with the pyramids for burying the corpse of a pharaoh, used the pretext that the pharaoh's corpse occupied only a niche, and had the pyramids blown up.

He would have blown up at the same time the whole magical and philosophical system for which the niche was only the point of departure and the corpse the condition.

On the other hand, the director who takes pains with his set to the detriment of the text is wrong, though perhaps less wrong than the critic who condemns his single-minded concern for the *mise en scène*.

For by taking pains with the *mise en scène*, which in a play is the truly and specifically theatrical part of the spectacle, the director hews to theater's true line, which is a matter of production. But both parties are playing with words; for if the term *mise en scène* has taken on, through usage, this deprecatory sense, it is a result of our European conception of the theater which gives precedence to spoken language over all other means of expression.

It has not been definitively proved that the language of words is the best possible language. And it seems that on the stage, which is above all a space to fill and a place where something happens, the language of words may have to give way before a language of *signs* whose objective aspect is the one that has the most immediate impact upon us.

Considered in this light, the objective work of the *mise en scène* assumes a kind of intellectual dignity from the effacement of words behind gestures and from the fact that the esthetic, plastic part of theater drops its role of decorative intermediary in order to become, in the proper sense of the word, a directly communicative *language*.

In other terms, if it is true that in a play made to be spoken, the director is wrong to wander off into stage effects more or less cleverly lit, interplay of groups, muted movements, all of which could be called epidermal effects which merely inflate the text, he is, in doing this, still closer to the concrete reality of theater than the author who might have confined himself to his text without recourse to the stage, whose spatial necessities seem to escape him.

Someone may point out here the high dramatic value of all the great tragedians, among whom it is certainly the literary or at any rate the spoken aspect that seems to dominate.

I shall answer that if we are clearly so incapable today of giving an idea of Aeschylus, Sophocles, Shakespeare that is worthy of them, it is probably because we have lost the sense of their theater's physics. It is because the directly human and active aspect of their way of speaking and moving, their whole scenic rhythm, escapes us. An aspect that ought to have as much if not more importance than the admirable spoken dissection of their heroes' psychology.

By this aspect, by means of this precise gesticulation which modifies itself through history we can rediscover the deep humanity of their theater.

But even if this physics really existed, I would still assert that none of these great tragedians is the theater itself, which is a matter of scenic materialization and which lives only by materialization. Let it be said, if one wishes, that theater is an inferior art—take a look around!—but theater resides in a certain way of furnishing and animating the air of the stage, by a conflagration of feelings and human sensations at a given point, creating situations that are expressed in concrete gestures.

Furthermore these concrete gestures must have an efficacy strong enough to make us forget the very necessity of speech. Then if spoken language still exists it must be only as a response, a relay stage of racing space; and the cement of gestures must by its human efficacy achieve the value of a true abstraction.

In a word, the theater must become a sort of experimental demonstration of the profound unity of the concrete and the abstract.

For beside the culture of words there is the culture of gestures. There are other languages in the world besides our Occidental language which has decided in favor of the despoiling and dessication of ideas, presenting them inert and unable to stir up in their course a whole system of natural analogies, as in Oriental languages.

The theater still remains the most active and efficient *site of passage* for those immense analogical disturbances in which ideas are arrested in flight at some point in their transmutation into the abstract.

There can be no complete theater which does not take account of these cartilaginous transformations of ideas; which does not add to our fully known feelings the expression of states of mind belonging to the half-conscious realm, which the suggestions of gestures will always express more adequately than the precise localized meanings of words.

It seems, in brief, that the highest possible idea of the theater is one that reconciles us philosophically with Becoming, suggesting to us through all sorts of objective situations the furtive idea of the passage and transmutation of ideas into things, much more than the transformation and stumbling of feelings into words.

It seems also that it was with just such an intention that the theater was created, to include man and his appetites only to the degree that he is magnetically confronted with his destiny. Not to submit to it, but to measure himself against it.

### SECOND LETTER

*To J. P.*                                          *Paris, September 28, 1932*

Dear friend,

I do not believe that if you had once read my Manifesto you could persevere in your objections, so either you have not read it or you have read it badly. My plays have nothing to do with Copeau's improvisations. However thoroughly they are immersed in the concrete and external, however rooted in free nature and not in the narrow chambers of the brain, they are not, for all that, left to the caprice of the wild and thoughtless inspiration of the actor, especially the modern actor who, once cut off from the text, plunges in without any idea of what he is doing. I would not care to leave the fate of my plays and of the theater to that kind of chance. No.

Here is what is really going to happen. It is simply a matter of changing the point of departure of artistic creation and of overturning the customary laws of the theater. It is a matter of substituting for the spoken language a different language of nature, whose expressive possibilities will be equal to verbal language, but whose source will be tapped at a point still deeper, more remote from thought.

The grammar of this new language is still to be found. Gesture is its material and its wits; and, if you will, its alpha and omega. It springs from the NECESSITY of speech more than from speech already formed. But finding an impasse in speech, it returns spontaneously to gesture. In passing, it touches upon some of the physical laws of human expression. It is immersed in necessity. It retraces poetically the path that has culminated in the creation of language. But with a manifold awareness of the worlds set in motion by the language of speech, which it revives in all their aspects. It brings again into the light all the relations fixed and enclosed in the strata of the human syllable, which has killed them by confining them. All the operations through which the word has passed in order to come to stand for that fiery Light-Bringer, whose Father Fire guards us like a shield in the form of Jupiter, the Latin contraction of Zeus-Pater—all these operations by means of cries, onomatopoeia, signs, attitudes, and by slow, copious, impassioned modulations of tension, level by level, term by term—these it recreates. For I make it my principle that words do not mean everything and that by their nature and defining character, fixed once and for all, they arrest and paralyze thought instead of permitting it and fostering its development. And by development I mean actual extended concrete qualities, so long as we are in an extended concrete world. The language of the theater aims then at encompassing and utilizing extension, that is to say space, and by utilizing it, to make it speak: I deal with objects—the data of extension —like images, like words, bringing them together and making them respond to each other according to laws of symbolism and living analogies: eternal laws, those of all poetry and all viable language, and, among other things, of Chinese ideograms and ancient Egyptian hieroglyphs. Hence, far from restricting the possibilities of theater and language, on the pretext that I will not perform written plays, I extend the language of the stage and multiply its possibilities.

I am adding another language to the spoken language, and I am trying to restore to the language of speech its old magic, its essential spellbinding power, for its mysterious possibilities have been forgotten. When I say I will perform no written play, I mean that I will perform no play based on writing and speech, that in the spectacles I produce there will be a preponderant physical share which could not be captured and written down in the customary language of words, and that even the spoken and written portions will be spoken and written in a new sense.

Theater which is the reverse of what is practiced here, i.e., in Europe, or better, in the Occident, will no longer be based on dialogue; and dialogue itself, the little that will remain, will not be written out and fixed a priori, but will be put on the stage, created on the stage, in correlation with the requirements of attitudes, signs, movements and objects. But this whole method of feeling one's way objectively among one's materials, in which Speech will appear as a necessity, as the result of a series of compressions, collisions, scenic frictions, evolutions of all kinds (thus the theater will become once more an authentic living operation, it will maintain that sort of emotional pulsation without which art is gratuitous)—all these gropings, researches, and shocks will culminate nevertheless in a work *written down*, fixed in its least details, and recorded by new means of notation. The composition, the creation, instead of being made in the brain of an author, will be made in nature itself, in real space, and the final result will be as strict and as calculated as that of any written work whatsoever, with an immense objective richness as well.

P.S.—The author must discover and assume what belongs to the *mise en scène* as well as what belongs to the author, and become a director himself in a way that will put a stop to the absurd duality existing between director and author.

An author who does not handle the scenic material directly and who does not move about the stage in orienting himself and making the power of his orientation serve the spectacle, has in reality betrayed his mission. And it is right for the actor to replace him. But so much the worse for the theater which is forced to suffer this usurpation.

Theatrical time, which is based upon breath, sometimes rushes by in great, consciously willed exhalations, sometimes contracts and attenuates to a prolonged feminine inhalation. An arrested gesture sets off a frantic complex seething, and this gesture bears within itself the magic of its evocation.

But though it may please us to offer suggestions concerning the energetic and animated life of the theater, we would not care to lay down laws.

Most certainly the human breath has principles which are all based upon innumerable combinations of the cabalistic ternaries. There are six principal ternaries but innumerable combinations, since it is from them that all life issues. And the theater is precisely the place where this magic respiration is reproduced at will. If the fixation of a major gesture requires around it a sharp and rapid breathing, this same exaggerated breathing can come to make its waves break slowly around a fixed gesture. There are abstract principles but no concrete plastic law; the only law is the poetic energy that proceeds from the stifled silence to the headlong representation of a spasm, and from individual speech *mezzo voce* to the weighty and resonant storm of a chorus slowly swelling its volume.

But the important thing is to create stages and perspectives from one language to the other. The secret of theater in space is dissonance, dispersion of timbres, and the dialectic discontinuity of expression.

The person who has an idea of what this language is will be able to understand us. We write only for him. We give elsewhere some supplementary particulars which complete the first Manifesto of the Theater of Cruelty.

Everything essential having been said in the first Manifesto, the second aims only at specifying certain points. It gives a workable definition of Cruelty and offers a description of scenic space. It remains to be seen what we make of it.


### THIRD LETTER

*To J. P.*                                    *Paris, November 9, 1932*

Dear friend,

Objections have been made to you and to me against the Manifesto of the Theater of Cruelty, some having to do with cruelty, whose function in my theater seems unclear, at least as an essential, determining element; others having to do with the theater as I conceive it.

As for the first objection, those who make it are right, not in relation to cruelty, nor in relation to the theater, but in relation to the place this cruelty occupies in my theater. I should have specified the very particular use I make of this word, and said that I employ it not in an episodic, accessory sense, out of a taste for sadism and perversion of mind, out of love of sensationalism and unhealthy attitudes, hence not at all in a circumstantial sense; it is not at all a matter of vicious cruelty, cruelty bursting with perverse appetites and expressing itself in bloody gestures, sickly excrescences upon an already contaminated flesh, but on the contrary, a pure and detached feeling, a veritable movement of the mind based on the gestures of life itself; the idea being that life, metaphysically speaking, because it admits extension, thickness, heaviness, and matter, admits, as a direct consequence, evil and all that is inherent in evil, space, extension and matter. All this culminates in consciousness and torment, and in consciousness *in* torment. Life cannot help exercising some blind rigor that carries with it all its conditions, otherwise it would not be life; but this rigor, this life that exceeds all bounds and is exercised in the torture and trampling down of everything, this pure implacable feeling is what cruelty is.

I have therefore said "cruelty" as I might have said "life" or "necessity," because I want to indicate especially that for me the theater is act and perpetual emanation, that there is nothing congealed about it, that I turn it into a true act, hence living, hence magical.

And I am searching for every technical and practical means of bringing the theater close to the high, perhaps excessive, at any rate vital and violent idea that I conceive of it for myself.

As for the drawing up of the Manifesto, I realize that it is abrupt and in large measure inadequate.

I propose unexpected, rigorous principles, of grim and terrible aspect, and just when everyone is waiting for me to justify them, I pass on to the next principle.

The dialectic of this Manifesto is admittedly weak. I leap without transition from one idea to another. No internal necessity justifies the arrangement.

As for the last objection, I claim that the director, having become a kind of demiurge, at the back of whose head is this idea of implacable purity and of its consummation whatever the cost, if he truly wants to be a director, i.e., a man versed in the nature of matter and objects, must conduct in the physical domain an exploration of intense movement and precise emotional gesture which is equivalent on the psychological level to the most absolute and complete moral discipline and on the cosmic level to the unchaining of certain blind forces which activate what they must activate and crush and burn on their way what they must crush and burn.

And here is the general conclusion.

Theater is no longer an art; or it is a useles art. It conforms at every point to the Occidental idea of art. We are surfeited with ineffectual decorative feelings and activities without aim, uniquely devoted to the pleasurable and the picturesque; we want a theater that functions actively, but on a level still to be defined.

We need true action, but without practical consequence. It is not on the social level that the action of theater unfolds. Still less on the moral and psychological levels.

Clearly the problem is not simple; but however chaotic, impenetrable, and forbidding our Manifesto may be, at least it does not evade the real question but on the contrary attacks it head on, which no one in the theater has dared to do for a long time. Nobody up to now has tackled the very principle of the theater, which is metaphysical; and if there are so few worthy plays, it is not for lack of talent or authors.

Putting the question of talent aside, there is a fundamental error of principle in the European theater; and this error is contingent upon a whole order of things in which the absence of talent appears as a consequence and not merely an accident.

If the age turns away from the theater, in which it is no longer interested, it is because the theater has ceased to represent it. It no longer hopes to be provided by the theater with Myths on which it can sustain itself.

We are living through a period probably unique in the history of the world, when the world, passed through a sieve, sees its old values crumble. Our calcined life is dissolving at its base, and on the moral or social level this is expressed by a monstrous unleashing of appetites, a liberation of the basest instincts, a crackling of burnt lives prematurely exposed to the flame.

What is interesting in the events of our time is not the events themselves, but this state of moral ferment into which they make our spirits fall; this extreme tension. It is the state of conscious chaos into which they ceaselessly plunge us.

And everything that disturbs the mind without causing it to lose its equilibrium is a moving means of expressing the innate pulsations of life.

It is from this mythical and moving immediacy that the theater has turned away; no wonder the public turns away from a theater that ignores actuality to this extent.

The theater as we practice it can therefore be reproached with a terrible lack of imagination. The theater must make itself the equal of life—not an individual life, that individual aspect of life in which CHARACTERS triumph, but the sort of liberated life which sweeps away human individuality and in which man is only a reflection. The true purpose of the theater is to create Myths, to express life in its immense, universal aspect, and from that life to extract images in which we find pleasure in discovering ourselves.

And by so doing to arrive at a kind of general resemblance, so powerful that it produces its effect instantaneously.

May it free *us,* in a Myth in which we have sacrificed our little human individuality, like Personages out of the Past, with powers rediscovered in the Past.

FOURTH LETTER

*To J. P.*                                    *Paris, May 28, 1933*

Dear friend,

I did not say that I wanted to act directly upon our times; I said that the theater I wanted to create assumed, in order to be possible, in order to be permitted by the times to exist, another form of civilization.

But without representing its times, the theater can impel the ideas, customs, beliefs, and principles from which the spirit of the time derives to a profound transformation. In any case it does not prevent me from doing what I want to do and doing it rigorously. I will do what I have dreamed or I will do nothing.

In the matter of the spectacle it is not possible for me to give supplementary particulars. And for two reasons:

1. the first is that for once what I want to do is easier to do than to say.

2. the second is that I do not want to risk being plagiarized, which has happened to me several times.

In my view no one has the right to call himself author, that is to say creator, except the person who controls the direct handling of the stage. And exactly here is the vulnerable point of the theater as it is thought of not only in France but in Europe and even in the Occident as a whole: Occidental theater recognizes as language, assigns the faculties and powers of a language, permits to be called language (with that particular intellectual dignity generally ascribed to this word) only articulated language, grammatically articulated language, i.e., the language of speech, and of written speech, speech which, pronounced or unpronounced, has no greater value than if it is merely written.

In the theater as we conceive it, the text is everything. It is understood and definitely admitted, and has passed into our habits and thinking, it is an established spiritual value that the language of words is *the* major language. But it must be admitted even from the Occidental point of view that speech becomes ossified and that words, all words, are frozen and cramped in their meanings, in a restricted schematic terminology. For the theater as it is practiced here, a written word has as much value as the same word spoken. To certain theatrical

amateurs this means that a play read affords just as definite
and as great a satisfaction as the same play performed. Everything concerning the particular enunciation of a word and the
vibration it can set up in space escapes them, and consequently,
everything that it is capable of adding to the thought. A word
thus understood has little more than a discursive, i.e., elucida-
tive, value. And it is not an exaggeration to say that in view of
its very definite and limited terminology the word is used only
to sidestep thought; it encircles it, but terminates it; it is only
a conclusion.

Obviously it is not without cause that poetry has abandoned
the theater. It is not merely an accident that for a very long
time now every dramatic poet has ceased to produce. The
language of speech has its laws. We have become too well
accustomed, for more than four hundred years, especially in
France, to employing words in the theater in a single defined
sense. We have made the action turn too exclusively on psychological themes whose essential combinations are not infinite, far from it. We have overaccustomed the theater to a
lack of curiosity and above all of imagination.

Theater, like speech, needs to be set free.

This obstinacy in making characters talk about feelings,
passions, desires, and impulses of a strictly psychological order, in which a single word is to compensate for innumerable
gestures, is the reason, since we are in the domain of precision,
the theater has lost its true *raison d'être* and why we have
come to long for a silence in it in which we could listen more
closely to life. Occidental psychology is expressed in dialogue;
and the obsession with the defined word which says everything
ends in the withering of words.

Oriental theater has been able to preserve a certain expansive value in words, since the defined sense of a word is not
everything, for there is its music, which speaks directly to the
unconscious. That is why in the Oriental theater there is no
spoken language, but a language of gestures, attitudes, and

signs which from the point of view of thought in action have as much expansive and revelational value as the other. And since in the Orient this sign language is valued more than the other, immediate magic powers are attributed to it. It is called upon to address not only the mind but the senses, and through the senses to attain still richer and more fecund regions of the sensibility at full tide.

If, then, the author is the man who arranges the language of speech and the director is his slave, there is merely a question of words. There is here a confusion over terms, stemming from the fact that, for us, and according to the sense generally attributed to the word *director*, this man is merely an artisan, an adapter, a kind of translator eternally devoted to making a dramatic work pass from one language into another; this confusion will be possible and the director will be forced to play second fiddle to the author only so long as there is a tacit agreement that the language of words is superior to others and that the theater admits none other than this one language.

But let there be the least return to the active, plastic, respiratory sources of language, let words be joined again to the physical motions that gave them birth, and let the discursive, logical aspect of speech disappear beneath its affective, physical side, i.e., let words be heard in their sonority rather than be exclusively taken for what they mean grammatically, let them be perceived as movements, and let these movements themselves turn into other simple, direct movements as occurs in all the circumstances of life but not sufficiently with actors on the stage, and behold! the language of literature is reconstituted, revivified, and furthermore—as in the canvasses of certain painters of the past—objects themselves begin to speak. Light, instead of decorating, assumes the qualities of an actual language, and the stage effects, all humming with significations, take on an order, reveal patterns. And this immediate and physical language is entirely at the director's disposal. This is the occasion for him to create in complete autonomy.

It would be quite singular if the person who rules a domain closer to life than the author's, i.e., the director, had on every occasion to yield precedence to the author, who by definition works in the abstract, i.e., on paper. Even if the *mise en scène* did not have to its credit the language of gestures which equals and surpasses that of words, any mute *mise en scène*, with its movement, its many characters, lighting, and set, should rival all that is most profound in paintings such as van den Leyden's "Daughters of Lot," certain "Sabbaths" of Goya, certain "Resurrections" and "Transfigurations" of Greco, the "Temptation of Saint Anthony" by Hieronymus Bosch, and the disquieting and mysterious "Dulle Griet" by the elder Breughel, in which a torrential red light, though localized in certain parts of the canvas, seems to surge up from all sides and, through some unknown technical process, glue the spectator's staring eyes while still yards away from the canvas: the theater swarms in all directions. The turmoil of life, confined by a ring of white light, runs suddenly aground on nameless shallows. A screeching, livid noise rises from this bacchanal of grubs of which even the bruises on human skin can never approach the color. Real life is moving and white; the hidden life is livid and fixed, possessing every possible attitude of incalculable immobility. This is mute theater, but one that tells more than if it had received a language in which to express itself. Each of these paintings has a double sense, and beyond its purely pictorial qualities discloses a message and reveals mysterious or terrible aspects of nature and mind alike.

But happily for the theater, the *mise en scène* is much more than that. For besides creating a performance with palpable material means, the pure *mise en scène* contains, in gestures, facial expressions and mobile attitudes, through a concrete use of music, everything that speech contains and has speech at its disposal as well. Rhythmic repetitions of syllables and particular modulations of the voice, swathing the precise sense of words, arouse swarms of images in the brain, producing a more or less hallucinatory state and impelling the sensibility and mind alike to a kind of organic alteration which helps to strip from the written poetry the gratuitousness that commonly characterizes it. And it is around this gratuitousness that the whole problem of theater is centered.

# XI. The Theater of Cruelty (Second Manifesto)

Admittedly or not, conscious or unconscious, the poetic state, a transcendent experience of life, is what the public is fundamentally seeking through love, crime, drugs, war, or insurrection.

The Theater of Cruelty has been created in order to restore to the theater a passionate and convulsive conception of life, and it is in this sense of violent rigor and extreme condensation of scenic elements that the cruelty on which it is based must be understood.

This cruelty, which will be bloody when necessary but not systematically so, can thus be identified with a kind of severe moral purity which is not afraid to pay life the price it must be paid.

## 1. FROM THE POINT OF VIEW OF CONTENT

that is, of the subjects and themes to be treated:

The Theater of Cruelty will choose subjects and themes corresponding to the agitation and unrest characteristic of our epoch.

It does not intend to leave the task of distributing the Myths of man and modern life entirely to the movies. But it will do it in its own way: that is, by resisting the economic, utilitarian. and technical streamlining of the world, it will again bring into fashion the great preoccupations and great essential passions which the modern theater has hidden under the patina of the pseudocivilized man.

These themes will be cosmic, universal, and interpreted according to the most ancient texts drawn from old Mexican, Hindu, Judaic, and Iranian cosmogonies.

Renouncing psychological man, with his well-dissected character and feelings, and social man, submissive to laws and misshapen by religions and precepts, the Theater of Cruelty will address itself only to total man.

And it will cause not only the recto but the verso of the mind to play its part; the reality of imagination and dreams will appear there on equal footing with life.

Furthermore, great social upheavals, conflicts between peoples and races, natural forces, interventions of chance, and the magnetism of fatality will manifest themselves either indirectly, in the movement and gestures of characters enlarged to the statures of gods, heroes, or monsters, in mythical dimensions, or directly, in material forms obtained by new scientific means.

These gods or heroes, these monsters, these natural and cosmic forces will be interpreted according to images from the most ancient sacred texts and old cosmogonies.

## 2. FROM THE POINT OF VIEW OF FORM

Besides this need for the theater to steep itself in the springs of an eternally passionate and sensuous poetry available to even the most backward and inattentive portions of the public, a poetry realized by a return to the primitive Myths, we shall require of the *mise en scène* and not of the text the task of materializing these old conflicts and above all of giving them *immediacy;* i.e., these themes will be borne directly into the theater and materialized in movements, expressions, and gestures before trickling away in words.

Thus we shall renounce the theatrical superstition of the text and the dictatorship of the writer.

And thus we rejoin the ancient popular drama, sensed and experienced directly by the mind without the deformations of language and the barrier of speech.

We intend to base the theater upon spectacle before everything else, and we shall introduce into the spectacle a new notion of space utilized on all possible levels and in all degrees of perspective in depth and height, and within this notion a specific idea of time will be added to that of movement:

In a given time, to the greatest possible number of movements, we will join the greatest possible number of physical images and meanings attached to those movements.

The images and movements employed will not be there solely for the external pleasure of eye or ear, but for that more secret and profitable one of the spirit.

Thus, theater space will be utilized not only in its dimensions and volume but, so to speak, *in its undersides (dans ses dessous)*.

The overlapping of images and movements will culminate, through the collusion of objects, silences, shouts, and rhythms, or in a genuine physical language with signs, not words, as its root.

For it must be understood that in this quantity of movements and images arranged for a given length of time, we include both silence and rhythm as well as a certain physical vibration and commotion, composed of objects and gestures really made and really put to use. And it can be said that the spirit of the most ancient hieroglyphs will preside at the creation of this pure theatrical language.

Every popular audience has always loved direct expressions and images; articulate speech, explicit verbal expressions will enter in all the clear and sharply elucidated parts of the action, the parts where life is resting and consciousness intervenes.

But in addition to this logical sense, words will be construed in an incantational, truly magical sense—for their shape and their sensuous emanations, not only for their meaning.

For these exciting appearances of monsters, debauches of heroes and gods, plastic revelations of forces, explosive interjections of a poetry and humor poised to disorganize and pulverize appearances, according to the anarchistic principle of all genuine poetry—these appearances will not exercise their true magic except in an atmosphere of hypnotic suggestion in which the mind is affected by a direct pressure upon the senses.

Whereas, in the digestive theater of today, the nerves, that is to say a certain physiological sensitivity, are deliberately left aside, abandoned to the individual anarchy of the spectator, the Theater of Cruelty intends to reassert all the time-tested magical means of capturing the sensibility.

These means, which consist of intensities of colors, lights, or sounds, which utilize vibration, tremors, repetition, whether of a musical rhythm or a spoken phrase, special tones or a general diffusion of light, can obtain their full effect only by the use of *dissonances*.

But instead of limiting these dissonances to the orbit of a single sense, we shall cause them to overlap from one sense to the other, from a color to a noise, a word to a light, a fluttering gesture to a flat tonality of sound, etc.

So composed and so constructed, the spectacle will be extended, by elimination of the stage, to the entire hall of the theater and will scale the walls from the ground up on light catwalks, will physically envelop the spectator and immerse him in a constant bath of light, images, movements, and noises. The set will consist of the characters themselves, enlarged to the stature of gigantic manikins, and of landscapes of moving lights playing on objects and masks in perpetual interchange.

And just as there will be no unoccupied point in space, there will be neither respite nor vacancy in the spectator's mind or sensibility. That is, between life and the theater there will be no distinct division, but instead a continuity. Anyone who has watched a scene of any movie being filmed will understand exactly what we mean.

We want to have at our disposal, for a theater spectacle, the same material means which, in lights, extras, resources of all kinds, are daily squandered by companies on whom everything that is active and magical in such a deployment is forever lost.

The first spectacle of the Theater of Cruelty will be entitled:

### THE CONQUEST OF MEXICO

It will stage events, not men. Men will come in their turn with their psychology and their passions, but they will be taken as the emanation of certain forces and understood in the light of the events and historical fatality in which they have played their role.

This subject has been chosen:

1. Because of its immediacy and all the allusions it permits to problems of vital interest for Europe and the world.

From the historical point of view, *The Conquest of Mexico* poses the question of colonization. It revives in a brutal and implacable way the ever active fatuousness of Europe. It permits her idea of her own superiority to be deflated. It contrasts Christianity with much older religions. It corrects the false conceptions the Occident has somehow formed concerning paganism and certain natural religions, and it underlines with burning emotion the splendor and forever immediate poetry of the old metaphysical sources on which these religions are built.

2. By broaching the alarmingly immediate question of colonization and the right one continent thinks it has to enslave another, this subject questions the real superiority of certain

races over others and shows the inmost filiation that binds the genius of a race to particular forms of civilization. It contrasts the tyrannical anarchy of the colonizers to the profound moral harmony of the as yet uncolonized.

Further, by contrast with the disorder of the European monarchy of the time, based upon the crudest and most unjust material principles, it illuminates the organic hierarchy of the Aztec monarchy established on indisputable spiritual principles.

From the social point of view, it shows the peacefulness of a society which knew how to feed all its members and in which the Revolution had been accomplished from the very beginnings.

Out of this clash of moral disorder and Catholic monarchy with pagan order, the subject can set off unheard-of explosions of forces and images, sown here and there with brutal dialogues. Men battling hand to hand, bearing within themselves, like stigmata, the most opposed ideas.

The moral grounds and the immediacy of interest of such a spectacle being sufficiently stressed, let us emphasize the value as *spectacle* of the conflicts it will set upon the stage.

There are first of all the inner struggles of Montezuma, the divided king concerning whose motivations history has been unable to enlighten us.

His struggles and his symbolic discussion with the visual myths of astrology will be shown in an objective pictorial fashion.

Then, besides Montezuma, there are the crowd, the different social strata, the revolt of the people against destiny as represented by Montezuma, the clamoring of the unbelievers, the quibbling of the philosophers and priests, the lamentations of the poets, the treachery of the merchants and the bourgeoisie, the duplicity and profligacy of the women.

The spirit of the crowds, the breath of events will travel in material waves over the spectacle, fixing here and there certain lines of force, and on these waves the dwindling, rebellious, or despairing consciousness of individuals will float like straws.

Theatrically, the problem is to determine and harmonize these lines of force, to concentrate them and extract suggestive melodies from them.

These images, movements, dances, rites, these fragmented melodies and sudden turns of dialogue will be carefully recorded and described as far as possible with words, especially for the portions of the spectacle not in dialogue, the principle here being to record in codes, as on a musical score, what cannot be described in words.

* Here now is the structure of the spectacle according to the order in which it will unfold.

## Act One

### WARNING SIGNS

A tableau of Mexico in anticipation, with its cities, its countrysides, its caves of troglodytes, its Mayan ruins.

Objects evoking on a grand scale certain Spanish ex-votos and those bizarre landscapes that are enclosed in bottles or under glass bells.

Similarly the cities, monuments, countryside, forest, ruins and caves will be evoked—their appearance, disappearance, their form in relief—by means of lighting. The musical or pictorial means of emphasizing their forms, of catching their sharpness will be devised in the spirit of a secret lyricism, invisible to the spectator, and which will correspond to the inspiration of a poetry overflowing with whispers and suggestions.

Everything trembles and groans, like a shop-window in a

* This fuller development of Artaud's *The Conquest of Mexico* was not included in the French edition of *LeThéâtre et son Double*; it was first published in *La Nef*, March-April 1950, where the whole text was called "Potlatch of mighty hosts for their mighty guests." M.C.R.

hurricane. A landscape which senses the coming storm; objects, music, stuffs, lost dresses, shadows of wild horses pass through the air like distant meteors, like lightning on the horizon brimming with mirages as the wind pitches wildly along the ground in a lighting prophecying torrential, violent storms. Then the lighting begins to change, and to the bawling conversations, the disputes between all the echoes of the population, respond the mute, concentrated, terrorized meetings of Montezuma with his formally assembled priests, with the signs of the zodiac, the austere forms of the firmament.

For Cortez, a *mise en scène* of sea and tiny battered ships, and Cortez and his men larger than the ships and firm as rocks.

## Act Two

### CONFESSION

Mexico seen this time by Cortez.

Silence concerning all his secret struggles; apparent stagnation and everywhere magic, magic of a motionless, unheard-of spectacle, with cities like ramparts of light, palaces on canals of stagnant water, a heavy melody.

Then suddenly, on a single sharp and piercing note, heads crown the walls.

Then a muffled rumbling full of threats, an impression of terrible solemnity, holes in the crowds like pockets of calm in a tornado: Montezuma advances all alone toward Cortez.

## Act Three

### CONVULSIONS

At every level of the country, revolt.

At every level of Montezuma's consciousness, revolt.

Battleground in the mind of Montezuma, who debates with destiny.

Magic, magical *mise en scène* evoking the Gods.

Montezuma cuts the living space, rips it open like the sex of a woman in order to cause the invisible to spring forth.

The stage wall is stuffed unevenly with heads, throats; cracked, oddly broken melodies, and responses to these melodies, appear like stumps. Montezuma himself seems split in two, divided; with some parts of himself in half-light, others dazzling; with many hands coming out of his dress, with expressions painted on his body like a multiple portrait of consciousness, but from within the consciousness of Montezuma all the questions pass forth into the crowd.

The Zodiac, which formerly roared with all it beasts in the head of Montezuma, turns into a group of human passions made incarnate by the learned heads of the official spokesmen, brilliant at disputation—a group of secret plays during which the crowd, despite the circumstances, does not forget to sneer.

However, the real warriors make their sabers whine, whetting them on the houses. Flying ships cross a Pacific of purplish indigo, laden with the riches of fugitives, and in the other direction contraband weapons arrive on other flying vessels.

An emaciated man eats soup as fast as he can, with a presentiment that the siege is approaching the city, and as the rebellion breaks out, the stage space is gorged with a brawling mosaic where sometimes men, sometimes compact troops tightly pressed together, limb to limb, clash frenetically. Space is stuffed with whirling gestures, horrible faces, dying eyes, clenched fists, manes, breastplates, and from all levels of the scene fall limbs, breastplates, heads, stomachs like a hailstorm bombarding the earth with supernatural explosions.

### Act Four

#### ABDICATION

The abdication of Montezuma results in a strange and almost malevolent loss of assurance on the part of Cortez and his fighters. A specific discord arises over the discovery of treasure, seen like illusions in the corners of the stage. (This will be done with mirrors.)

Lights and sounds produce an impression of dissolving, unravelling, spreading, and squashing—like watery fruits splashing on the ground. Strange couples appear, Spaniard with Indian, horribly enlarged, swollen and black, swaying back and forth like carts about to overturn. Several Hernando Cortez's enter at the same time, signifying that there is no longer any leader. In some places, Indians massacre Spaniards; while in front of a statue whose head is revolving in time to music, Cortez, arms dangling, seems to dream. Treasons go unpunished, shapes swarm about, never exceeding a certain height in the air.

This unrest and the threat of a revolt on the part of the conquered will be expressed in ten thousand ways. And in this collapse and disintegration of the brutal force which has worn itself out (having nothing more to devour) will be delineated the first inkling of a passionate romance.

Weapons abandoned, emotions of lust now make their appearance. Not the dramatic passions of so many battles, but calculated feelings, a plot cleverly hatched, in which, for the first time in the spectacle, a woman's head will be manifested.

And as a consequence of all this, it is also the time of miasmas, of diseases.

On every expressive level appear, like muted flowerings: sounds, words, poisonous blooms which burst close to the ground. And, at the same time, a religious exhalation bends men's heads, fearful sounds seem to bray out, clear as the capricious flourishes of the sea upon a vast expanse of sand, of a cliff slashed by rocks. These are the funeral rites of Montezuma. A stamping, a murmur. The crowd of natives whose steps sound like a scorpion's jaws. Then, eddies in the path of the miasmas, enormous heads with noses swollen with the stink—and nothing, nothing but immense Spaniards on crutches. And like a tidal wave, like the sharp burst of a storm, like the whipping of rain on the sea, the revolt which carries off the whole crowd in groups, with the body of the dead Montezuma tossed on their heads like a ship. And the sharp spasms of the battle, the foam of heads of the cornered Spaniards who are squashed like blood against the ramparts that are turning green again.

# XII. An Affective Athleticism

One must grant the actor a kind of affective musculature which corresponds to the physical localizations of feelings.

The actor is like the physical athlete, but with this surprising difference: his affective organism is analogous to the organism of the athlete, is parallel to it, as if it were its double, although not acting upon the same plane.

The actor is an athlete of the heart.

The division of the total person into three worlds obtains also for him; and his is the affective sphere.

It belongs to him organically.

The muscular movements of physical effort comprise an effigy of another effort, their double, and in the movements of dramatic action are localized at the same points.

What the athlete depends upon in running is what the actor depends upon in shouting a passionate curse, but the actor's course is altogether interior.

All the tricks of wrestling, boxing, the hundred yard dash, high-jumping, etc., find analogous organic bases in the movement of the passions; they have the same physical points of support.

With however this additional correction, that the movement is reversed: in breathing, for example, the actor's body is supported by his breath whereas the physical athlete's breath is supported by his body.

This question of breath is in fact primary; it is in inverse proportion to the strength of the external expression.

The more sober and restrained the expression, the deeper and heavier the breathing, the more substantial and full of resonances.

Similarly an expression that is broad and full and externalized has a corresponding breath in short and broken waves.

It is certain that for every feeling, every mental action, every leap of human emotion there is a corresponding breath which is appropriate to it.

The tempos of the breath have a name taught us by the Cabala; it is these tempos which give the human heart its shape, and the movements of the passions their sex.

The actor is merely a crude empiricist, a practitioner guided by vague instinct.

However, it is not a matter, whatever one may think, of teaching him to be incoherent.

It is a matter of remedying this wild ignorance in which the whole contemporary theater moves as if in a fog, ceaselessly stumbling. The gifted actor finds by instinct how to tap and radiate certain powers; but he would be astonished indeed if it were revealed to him that these powers, which have their material trajectory by and *in the organs*, actually exist, for he has never realized they could actually exist.

To make use of his emotions as a wrestler makes use of his muscles, he has to see the human being as a Double, like the Ka of the Egyptian mummies, like a perpetual specter from which the affective powers radiate.

The plastic and never completed specter, whose forms the true actor apes, on which he imposes the forms and image of his own sensibility.

It is this double which the theater influences, this spectral effigy which it shapes, and like all specters, this double has a long memory. The heart's memory endures and it is certainly with his heart that the actor thinks; here the heart holds sway.

This means that in the theater more than anywhere else it is the affective world of which the actor must be aware, ascribing to it virtues which are not those of an image but carry a material sense.

Whether the hypothesis is exact or not, the important thing is that it is verifiable.

The soul can be physiologically reduced to a skein of vibrations.

This soul-specter can be regarded as intoxicated with its own screams, something like the Hindu *mantras*—those consonances, those mysterious accents, in which the material secrets of the soul, tracked down to their lairs, speak out in broad daylight.

The belief in a fluid materiality of the soul is indispensable to the actor's craft. To know that a passion is material, that it is subject to the plastic fluctuations of material, makes accessible an empire of passions that extends our sovereignty.

To join with the passions by means of their forces, instead of regarding them as pure abstractions, confers a mastery upon the actor which makes him equal to a true healer.

To know that the soul has a corporeal expression permits the actor to unite with this soul from the other side, and to rediscover its being by mathematical analogies.

To understand the secret of the passional time—a kind of musical *tempo* which regulates their harmonic beat—is an aspect of theater long undreamed of by our modern psychological theater.

This *tempo* can be discovered by analogy; and it is found in the six ways of apportioning and conserving the breath as if it were a precious element.

Every breath has three kinds of time, just as there are three principles at the root of all creation which find a corresponding pattern even in the breath.

The Cabala apportions the human breath into six principal arcana, the first of which, called the Great Arcanum, is that of creation:

| ANDROGYNOUS | MALE | FEMALE |
|---|---|---|
| BALANCED | EXPANDING | ATTRACTING |
| NEUTRAL | POSITIVE | NEGATIVE |

I have had the idea of employing this knowledge of the kinds of breathing not only in the actor's work but in the actor's preparation for his craft. For if knowledge of breathing makes clear the soul's color, it can with all the more reason stimulate the soul and encourage its blossoming.

It is certain that since breathing accompanies effort, the mechanical production of breath will engender in the working organism a quality corresponding to effort.

The effort will have the color and rhythm of the artificially produced breath.

Effort sympathetically accompanies breathing and, according to the quality of the effort to be produced, a preparatory emission of breath will make this effort easy and spontaneous. I insist on the word spontaneous, for breath rekindles life, sets it afire in its own substance.

What voluntary breathing provokes is a spontaneous reappearance of life. Like a voice, in infinite colors on the edges of which warriors lie sleeping. The morning reveille sends them by ranks into the thick of the fight. But let a child suddenly cry "Wolf!" and see how these same warriors leap up. They wake in the middle of the night. False alarm: the soldiers are beginning to return. But no: they run into hostile camps, they have fallen into a regular hornet's nest. It is in a dream that the child has cried out. Its more sensitive, fluctuating unconscious has stumbled into a troop of enemies. Thus by indirect means, the fiction provoked by the theater falls upon a reality much more forbidding than the other, a reality never suspected by life.

Thus with the whetted edge of breath the actor carves out his character.

For breath, which nourishes life, allows its stages to be ascended rung by rung. And an actor can arrive by means of breath at a feeling which he does not have, provided its effects are judiciously combined and its sex not mistaken. For breath is either male or female; and less often it is androgynous. However, one may have rare undeveloped states to depict.

Breath accompanies feeling, and the actor can penetrate into this feeling by means of breath provided he knows how to select among the different kinds the one appropriate to the feeling.

There are, as we have said, six principal combinations of breaths.

| | | |
|---|---|---|
| NEUTER | MASCULINE | FEMININE |
| NEUTER | FEMININE | MASCULINE |
| MASCULINE | NEUTER | FEMININE |
| FEMININE | NEUTER | MASCULINE |
| MASCULINE | FEMININE | NEUTER |
| FEMININE | MASCULINE | NEUTER |

And a seventh state which is beyond breath and which, through the door of the highest Guna, the state of Sattva, joins the manifest to the non-manifest.

If it is claimed that the actor should not be preoccupied with this seventh state since he is not essentially a metaphysician, we shall reply that even though the theater may be the perfect and most complete symbol of universal manifestation, the actor carries in himself the principle of that seventh state, of that blood-route by which he penetrates into all the others each time his organs in full power awaken from their sleep.

Indeed most of the time instinct is there to compensate for the absence of an idea that cannot be defined; and there is no need to fall from so high to emerge among median passions like those that stuff the contemporary theater. Moreover the system of breaths has not been invented to produce median passions. And our repeated exercises in breathing, developing its procedures by intense practice, are not cultivated merely to prepare us for a declaration of adulterous love.

But for a subtle quality of outcry, for the soul's desperate claims—it is for these that an emission of breath seven or twelve times repeated prepares us.

And we localize this breath, we apportion it out in states of contraction and release combined. We use our body like a screen through which pass the will and the relaxation of will.

The tempo of voluntary thought we project by a forcefully male beat, followed without too apparent a transition by a prolonged feminine beat.

The tempo of involuntary thought or even of no thought at all is expressed by a weary feminine breath that makes us inhale a stifling cellar heat, the moist wind of a forest; and on the same prolonged beat we exhale heavily; however the muscles of our whole body, vibrating by areas, have not ceased to function.

The important thing is to become aware of the localization of emotive thought. One means of recognition is effort or tension; and the same points which support physical effort are those which also support the emanation of emotive thought: they serve as a springboard for the emanation of a feeling.

It is to be noted that everything feminine—that which is surrender, anguish, plea, invocation—everything that stretches toward something in a gesture of supplication—is supported also upon the points where effort is localized, but like a diver pressing against the bottom of the sea in order to rise to the surface: it is as if emptiness gushes from the spot where the tension was.

But in this case the masculine returns to haunt the place of the feminine like a shadow; while, when the affective state is male, the interior body consists of a sort of inverse geometry, an image of the state reversed.

To become conscious of physical obsession of muscles quivering with affectivity, is equivalent, as in the play of breaths, to unleashing this affectivity in full force, giving it a mute but profound range of extraordinary violence.

Thus it appears that any actor whatsoever, even the least gifted, can by means of this physical knowledge increase the internal density and volume of his feeling, and a full-bodied expression follows upon this organic taking-hold.

It does no harm to our purposes to know certain points of localization.

The man who lifts weights lifts them with his back; it is by a contortion of his back that he supports the fortified strength of his arms; and curiously enough he claims that, inversely, when any feminine feeling hollows him out—sobbing, despair, spasmodic panting, dread—he realizes his emptiness in the small of his back, at the very place where Chinese acupuncture relieves congestion of the kidney. For Chinese medicine proceeds only by concepts of empty and full. Convex and concave. Tense and relaxed. *Yin* and *Yang*. Masculine and feminine.

Another radiating point: the location of anger, attack, biting is the center of the solar plexus. It is there that the head supports itself in order to cast its venom, morally speaking.

The location of heroism and sublimity is also that of guilt —where one strikes one's breast. The spot where anger boils, the anger that rages and does not advance.

But where anger advances, guilt retreats; that is the secret of the empty and the full.

A high-pitched, self-mutilating anger begins with a clacking neuter and is localized in the plexus by a rapid feminine emptying; then, obstructed by the two shoulder-blades, turns like a boomerang and erupts in male sparks, which consume themselves without going further. In order to lose their aggressive quality they preserve the correlation of male breath: they expire fiercely.

I have wanted to give only a few examples bearing on a few fertile principles which comprise the material of this technical essay. Others, if they have time, will prepare the complete anatomy of the system. There are 380 points in Chinese acupuncture, with 73 principal ones which are used in current therapy. There are many fewer crude outlets for human affectivity.

Many fewer supports which can be indicated and on which to base the soul's athleticism.

The secret is to exacerbate these supports as if one were flaying the muscles.

The rest is done by outcry.

In order to reforge the chain, the chain of a rhythm in which the spectator used to see his own reality in the spectacle, the spectator must be allowed to identify himself with the spectacle, breath by breath and beat by beat.

It is not sufficient for this spectator to be enchained by the magic of the play; it will not enchain him if we do not know *where to take hold of him*. There is enough chance magic, enough poetry which has no science to back it up.

In the theater, poetry and science must henceforth be identical.

Every emotion has organic bases. It is by cultivating his emotion in his body that the actor recharges his voltage.

To know in advance what points of the body to touch is the key to throwing the spectator into magical trances. And it is this invaluable kind of science that poetry in the theater has been without for a long time.

To know the points of localization in the body is thus to reforge the magical chain.

And through the hieroglyph of a breath I am able to recover an idea of the sacred theater.

N.B.—No one in Europe knows how to scream any more, and particularly actors in trance no longer know how to cry out. Since they do nothing but talk and have forgotten they ever had a body in the theater, they have naturally also forgotten the use of their windpipes. Abnormally shrunk, the windpipe is not even an organ but a monstrous abstraction that talks: actors in France no longer know how to do anything but talk.

# XIII. Two Notes

The first film of the Marx Brothers that we have seen here, *Animal Crackers*, appeared to me and to everyone as an *extraordinary thing*: the liberation through the medium of the screen of a particular magic which the customary relation of words and images does not ordinarily reveal, and if there is a definite characteristic, a distinct poetic state of mind that can be called *surrealism, Animal Crackers* participated in that state altogether.

It is difficult to say of what this kind of magic consists. It is probably not specifically cinematic, nor theatrical; perhaps only certain successful surrealist poems, if there were any, could give an idea of it. The poetic quality of a film like *Animal Crackers* would fit the definition of humor if this word had not long since lost its sense of essential liberation, of destruction of all reality in the mind.

In order to understand the powerful, total, definitive, absolute originality (I am not exaggerating, I am trying simply to define, and so much the worse if my enthusiasm carries me away) of films like *Animal Crackers* and, at times (at any rate in the whole last part), *Monkey Business,* you would have to add to humor the notion of something disquieting and tragic, a fatality (neither happy nor unhappy, difficult to

142

formulate) which would hover over it like the cast of an appalling malady upon an exquisitely beautiful profile.

In *Monkey Business* the Marx Brothers, each with his own style, are confident and ready, one feels, to wrestle with circumstances. Whereas in *Animal Crackers* each character was losing face from the very beginning, here for three-quarters of the picture one is watching the antics of clowns who are amusing themselves and making jokes, some very successful, and it is only at the end that things grow complicated, that objects, animals, sounds, master and servants, host and guests, everything goes mad, runs wild, and revolts amid the simultaneously ecstatic and lucid comments of one of the Marx Brothers, inspired by the spirit he has finally been able to unleash and whose stupefied and momentary commentator he seems to be. There is nothing at once so hallucinatory and so terrible as this type of man-hunt, this battle of rivals, this chase in the shadows of a cow barn, a stable draped in cobwebs, while men, women and animals break their bounds and land in the middle of a heap of crazy objects, each of whose *movement* or *noise* functions in its turn.

In *Animal Crackers* a woman may suddenly fall, legs in the air, on a divan and expose, for an instant, all we could wish to see—a man may throw himself abruptly upon a woman in a salon, dance a few steps with her and then whack her on the behind in time to the music—these events comprise a kind of exercise of intellectual freedom in which the unconscious of each of the characters, repressed by conventions and habits, avenges itself and us at the same time. But in *Monkey Business* when a hunted man throws himself upon a beautiful woman and dances with her, *poetically,* in a sort of study in charm and grace of attitude, the spiritual claim seems double and shows everything that is poetic and revolutionary in the Marx Brothers' jokes.

But the fact that the music to which the couple dances —the hunted man and the beautiful woman—may be a music of nostalgia and escape, *a music of deliverance,* sufficiently indicates the dangerous aspect of all these funny jokes; and when the poetic spirit is exercised, it always leads toward a kind of boiling anarchy, an essential disintegration of the real by poetry.

If Americans, to whose spirit (*esprit*) this genre of films belongs, wish to take these films in a merely humorous sense, confining the material of humor to the easy comic margins of the meaning of the word, so much the worse for them; but that will not prevent us from considering the conclusion of *Monkey Business* as a hymn to anarchy and wholehearted revolt, this ending that puts the bawling of a calf on the same intellectual level and gives it the same quality of meaningful suffering as the scream of a frightened woman, this ending that shows, in the shadows of a dirty barn, two lecherous servants freely pawing the naked shoulders of their master's daughter, the equals at last of their hysterical master, all amidst the intoxication—which is intellectual as well—of the Marx Brothers' pirouettes. And the triumph of all this is in the kind of exaltation, simultaneously visual and sonorous, to which these events attain among the shadows, in their intensity of vibration, and in the powerful anxiety which their total effect ultimately projects into the mind.

## II. AUTOUR D'UNE MERE *

### *A Dramatic Action by Jean-Louis Barrault*

In Jean-Louis Barrault's spectacle there is a sort of marvelous *centaur-horse,* and our emotion before it was as great as

* Mime created by Jean-Louis Barrault, based on William Faulkner's *As I Lay Dying,* and first performed at the end of the 1934-35 season. M.C.R.

if J.-L. Barrault had restored magic itself to us with the entrance of his *centaur-horse*.

This spectacle is magical like those incantations of witch doctors when the clackings of their tongues against their palates bring rain to a countryside; when, before the exhausted sick man, the witch doctor gives his breath the form of a strange disease, and chases away the sickness with his breath. In the same way, in J.-L. Barrault's spectacle, at the moment of the mother's death, a chorus of screams comes to life.

I do not know if such a success is a masterpiece; in any case it is an event. When an atmosphere is so transformed that a hostile audience is suddenly and blindly immersed and invincibly disarmed, it must be hailed as an event.

There is a secret strength in this spectacle which wins the public like a great love wins a soul ripe for rebellion.

A great, young love, a youthful vigor, a spontaneous and lively effervescence flow through the disciplined movements and stylized mathematical gestures like the twittering of birds through colonnades of trees in a magically arranged forest.

It is here, in this sacred atmosphere, that Jean-Louis Barrault improvises the movements of a wild horse, and that one is suddenly amazed to see him turn into a horse.

His spectacle demonstrates the irresistible expressiveness of gesture; it victoriously proves the importance of gesture and of movement in space. He restores to theatrical perspective the importance it should never have lost. He fills the stage with emotion and life.

It is in relation to the stage and *on* the stage that this spectacle is organized: it cannot live except on the stage. And there is not one point in the stage perspective that does not take on emotional meaning.

In the animated gesticulations and discontinuous unfolding of images there is a kind of direct physical appeal, something as convincing as solace itself, and which memory will never release.

Nor will it release the mother's death nor her screams re-echoing in space and time, the epic crossing of the river, the fire rising in men's throats and corresponding, on the level of gesture, to the rising of another fire; and above all that man-horse running through the play, as if the very spirit of Fable had come down among us again.

Up to now only the Balinese Theater seemed to have kept a trace of this lost spirit.

What does it matter if Jean-Louis Barrault has restored the religious spirit by profane descriptive means, since every-thing that is authentic is sacred and since his gestures are so beautiful that they take on a symbolic significance.

Indeed, there are no symbols in Jean-Louis Barrault's play. And if any reproach can be made against his gestures, it is that they give us the illusion of symbol when in fact they are defining reality; and that is why their expression, however violent and active it may be, has no range beyond itself.

It has no such range because it is merely descriptive, because it describes facts in which souls do not intervene; because it does not touch the quick of either thoughts or souls. And it is here, rather than in the question of whether this form of theater is *theatrical,* that criticism of his work can be made.

But his work uses the means of the theater—for the theater, which opens up a physical field, requires that this field be filled, that its space be furnished with gestures, that this space live magically in itself, release within itself an aviary of sounds, and discover there new relations between sound, gesture, and voice—and therefore we can say that what J.-L. Barrault has done is theater.

But yet this performance is not the peak of theater, I mean the deepest drama, the mystery deeper than souls, the ex-cruciating conflict of souls where gesture is only a path—there where man is only a point and where lives drink at their source. But who has drunk at the sources of life?

# IN MEMORIAM: ANTONIN ARTAUD

Antonin Artaud died March 4, 1948, at the age of fifty-two. The date should be remembered as that of a new and terrible birth: the moment this body and this mind, riveted together by long agony, parted company, Artaud's *real life* began. The hailstorm of his thought now batters our own; the harp of his nerves vibrates in the world's void; and the knell has rung for several transitory forms of literature and art.

In 1922, when his first poems were published in the *Mercure de France* ("*La Marée*," "*Marine*," and "*Soir*"), Artaud was still the "gentle angel" being murdered in slow motion that same year in Claude Autant-Lara's film *Fait-Divers*. His face and his poetry were instinct with that disturbing gentleness of a soul torn between heaven and hell, a soul that can find the meaning and fulfillment of its perfection only in its own disaster. The symbolist cult of the spiritual, its preoccupation with "obscure matters" is evident in Artaud's preface to Maeterlinck's *Douze Chansons*, in which he also praises Boehme, Novalis, and Ruysbroek: this is the period of his own mystical poems and of *Tric-Trac du Ciel*. It is also the period in which he was acting with Dullin, who permitted him to direct Calderon's *Life Is a Dream*. He studied the Elizabethan theater which spattered gold and blood upon the

lofty clouds of his own aspirations as a poet. And he seems
to have found his vocation when he writes: "Drama is the
mind's most perfect expression. It is in the nature of profound
things to clash and combine, to evolve from one another.
Action is the very principle of life."

Nor is there much doubt that he was already familiar with
those "sacred poisons" which were to mark his life as they
had Baudelaire's. In 1923 he showed someone he knew to
be interested in new forms of expression a slender notebook
of poems—all or almost all in praise of morphine. Perhaps
these were the same poems he sent to the editor of the *Nouvelle Revue Française*, poems which were to lead to the
*Correspondance avec Jacques Rivière*, an essential document
in the history of modern literature, a document which pro-
pounds the drama of Antonin Artaud.

It is evident he made no mistake in his choice of a con-
fidant. With his extraordinary instinct for the secret resources
of the soul, an instinct he retained until the end of his life,
he sensed Rivière's "extreme sensitivity," his mind's "almost
morbid penetration." He therefore entrusted to Rivière his
very existence as a writer. At the same time he inquired about
the "absolute admissibility" of his poems, he presented himself as a mental case, an illustration of "fragility of mind":
"I suffer from a fearful mental disease. My ideas abandon
me at every stage, from the mere fact of thought itself to the
exterior phenomenon of its materialization in words. Words,
the forms of sentences, inner directions of thought, the mind's
simplest reactions:—I am in constant pursuit of my intellectual being."

The ambiguity of this letter, which is both a request for
literary advice and an examination of his own conscience
(as are the letters that follow), deceived Jacques Rivière as
to the quality of his correspondent. As to most young poets
who aspired to publication, he counselled patience and the
diligent pursuit of an original temperament—which, once

seized, would enable the young man to write "perfectly coherent and harmonious" poems.

But Antonin Artaud—perhaps unconsciously—had transcended literary questions of a purely formal nature. If he hoped for publication, it was to reassure himself about his ideas in terms of their initial value, rather than as ultimate productions. A few months later he felt the need to resume his confession in order to plumb, if possible, his inmost depths. What is striking is the distance—the elevation—he preserves, even in moments of the most extreme intimacy: "I always have the distance separating me from myself to cure me of other people's opinions." The defects—the diffusion—of his poems reveal, as he put it, "a collapse of the soul at its center, a kind of erosion [of ideas] that is both essential and fugitive." And he implored Rivière to be his rescuer or his absolute judge—while providing himself one loophole: "I am a man whose mind has suffered greatly, and as such I have the *right* to speak. I know how the mind's dealings are negotiated. I have agreed to yield once and for all to my inferiority. . . ."

Jacques Rivière was not to be disconcerted by the pride that mingled with the distress of this cry. He tried, sincerely enough, to locate Artaud's quest somewhere between the marvelous *mise en scène* of "our autonomous intellectual operations" which Valéry determined in *La Soirée avec M. Teste,* and the dawning temptations of surrealism: "There is a whole literature—I know it preoccupies you as much as it interests me—which is the product of the immediate and, so to speak, animal operation of the mind. This literature has the appearance of a great plain of ruins; the columns still standing are supported by chance alone. It is chance that reigns there, chance and a sort of dreary multiplicity."

Rivière protested against this excessive liberty granted to the mind—"the absolute is the source of our disorder"—and at the same time warned against the dangers involved in the absence of purpose or limit in the exercise of thought: "To become taut, the mind requires limitation, an encounter with the blessed opacity of experience. The only cure for madness is the innocence of facts."

It appears that Rivière was correct in his diagnosis of Artaud's inability to concentrate on an object. Is this disease —which his correspondent is conscious of sharing with so many others (he gives as examples Tristan Tzara, André Breton, Pierre Reverdy)—"something in the spirit of the times, a miracle floating in the air, a cosmic prodigy of evil, or is it the discovery of a new world, a genuine extension of reality?" Yet unlike his contemporaries, Artaud feels that his soul is "physiologically stricken." He is as unattached to life as to poetry. And he arrives quite logically at a position foreboding the most tragic self-renunciation to which a man has ever consented: "In me this want of application to an object, a characteristic of all literature, is a want of application to life. Speaking for myself, I can honestly say that I am not in the world, and that such a statement is not merely an intellectual attitude."

André Breton's theories were as impotent as Rivière's Christian charity and literary integrity to maintain or withstand the destiny of an Artaud. Today our total experience of this destiny judges and condemns surrealism, which has revealed itself as nothing more than a certain repertory of intellectual attitudes, or, more commonly, of attitudes *tout court*. Director of the Office of Surrealist Research in 1925, principal author of the Addresses to the Pope and the Dalai Lama, published in the third number of *La Révolution Surréaliste,* Artaud committed himself body and soul to a movement in which his comrades confined themselves to playing —elegantly enough—with fire. This is obvious if we compare his splendid *Lettre à la voyante* with the similar texts that abound in the surrealist books and magazines; if we read his letter about the narcotics law, his accounts of dreams, and his answers to various questionnaires on the subject of suicide (which, he felt, should be *anterior,* i.e., capable of making us turn back, "but on the other side of existence, and not on the side of death").

Artaud's relations with surrealism are doubtless of interest only to literary historians, or to literary gossips. They were inevitably "tempestuous" (like everything else that went on in those barracks) and quite discontinuous. It is worth remarking that Artaud never indulged in automatic writing, that elementary exercise which allowed the school's more talented members access to an undeniable poetic *verve,* but which was to become the most facile and monotonous of conventions. Artaud is one of the rare men of his generation who seriously tried to cut off his "writing hand," to break with the bundle of academic or surrealistic tricks that make it possible to fill a page or a book with the least possible effort and call it writing. He expressed himself on this subject with agreeable ferocity—which should all the same be taken quite literally:

"All writing is rubbish.

"People who try to free themselves from what is vague in order to state precisely whatever is going on in their minds are producing rubbish.

"The whole literary tribe is a pack of rubbish-mongers, especially today.

"All those who have landmarks in their minds, I mean in a certain part of their heads, in well-defined sites in their skulls, all those who are masters of language, all those for whom words have meaning, all those for whom the soul has its heights and thought its currents, those who are the spirits of the times, and who have given names to these currents of thought—I am thinking of their specific tasks, and of that mechanical creaking their minds produce at every gust of wind—are rubbish-mongers."

We have already seen how Artaud, in his correspondence with Jacques Rivière, made his farewells to intellectual life, properly speaking—yet without losing hope of expressing himself "in dense and active language." He achieved this language from the moment he gave up thinking of his mind as an autonomous organ. In *L'Ombilic des Limbes, Le Pèse-nerfs,* and *L'Art et la Mort,* which are so many "descriptions of a physical state," Artaud becomes detached and yet remains present in this mind identified with this body, this mind inter-mingled with this bundle of nerves—this mind which "has opened onto the belly, and accumulates from below a dark and untranslatable knowledge, full of subterranean tides, hollow structures, a congealed agitation." He is careful to add: "Do not construe these words as images. They are attempting to construct an abominable wisdom."

From this point on, Antonin Artaud observes Antonin Artaud. His work is an inventory of himself (for he refers everything back to his own body, which is a prey to the fires of his mind—whether his subject is Abelard, Uccello, or a painting by André Masson) and at the same time an intermi-nable message to himself. The being who *experiences* his limbs and his brain to this degree has no need to communicate with anyone else, and this separation was to grow worse year by year in Artaud, until he answered the call of madness itself.

Dreading this summons, he persisted in struggling against the dizziness he experienced in his own presence: "It seems to me I have plagued men enough with accounts of my spiritual limitations, my excruciating psychical inadequacy; I think they have a right to expect me either to offer some-thing more than impotent cries and the catalog of my short-comings, or else keep quiet." And he attempts, by means of the theater, to escape his own performance.

Facing the public, he becomes that strange movie actor we discover now in Abel Gance's *Napoléon* (his splenetic and rebellious Marat leaves us with one unforgettable image of the man after Charlotte Corday's crime—his head, sinister and yet seraphic, leaning on the edge of the bathtub); now in *La Passion de Jeanne d'Arc* (the most remarkable of his screen roles: Carl Dreyer put his beauty to marvelous use as the tempter monk who comes to the Maid not so much to confess her as to tear from her an admission of heresy); now in Pabst's *L'Opéra de Quat' Sous,* in which he plays the upper-class young man who joins the beggars. Apparently Artaud did not always choose his own parts: his participation in a number of "commercial" films between 1919 and 1932 suggests that he regarded the cinema chiefly as a means of livelihood. He also wrote two scenarios: *La Coquille et le Clergyman,* produced in 1926 by Germaine Dulac, and *La Révolte du Boucher.* In these efforts he attempted to work out a theory of a subjective and visual kind of cinema "in which even psychology would be devoured by the action."

This insistence on being "devoured by acts," this need for psychic and physical expenditure characterizes his many theatrical experiments, of which the first was a Théâtre Alfred Jarry, founded with Roger Vitrac, where he produced, between 1927 and 1929, Strindberg's *Dream Play,* the third act of Claudel's *Partage de Midi* (acted as a farce), several of Vitrac's plays, a musical sketch of his own, and Max Robur's *Gigogne* (produced "as an intentional provocation").

Yet Artaud's dreams were to have more effect in the theater than all his work as actor and director. Although he gave full measure of his discoveries and his talents in a production—and performance—of his play *Les Cenci,* a drama expressing all the ferocity and corruption of the Renaissance, modeled after the versions by Stendhal and Shelley, Artaud nevertheless remained for many years outside the actual world of the theatre, its companies and performances. Outside, but not apart: it was during these years that he wrote the manifestoes collected in 1938 in *Le Théâtre et son Double.*

The first of these, favoring a "Theater of Cruelty" and opening with this lapidary sentence: "We cannot go on prostituting the idea of theater, whose only value is in its excruciating, magical relation to reality and danger," reveals his preoccupations. Artaud wanted not to reform but to revolutionize dramatic art from top to bottom. Scorning all *literature* written to be performed ("No More Masterpieces"), all Western traditions ("On the Balinese Theater," "An Affective Athleticism"), and civilization itself ("The Theater and the Plague"), Artaud declares his willingness to destroy all forms of language and all social proprieties in order to bring life into the theater and make actors and spectators alike into "victims burnt at the stake, signaling through the flames."

Before following Artaud along a path for which the theater was perhaps only an *active* pretext, we must consider parenthetically two works he wrote "between the acts." These were the two demoniacal novels in which Artaud relates the lives of other Antonins, as Baudelaire would have liked to relate his own by translating Maturin's *Melmoth*. The first is in fact a French "copy" of M. G. Lewis's original *roman noir, The Monk*. In this supernatural debauch Artaud distinguishes ETERNAL LIFE and claims to believe it from beginning to end: "I have given myself over to charlatans, osteopaths, mages, wizards, and palmists because all these things *are,* and because, for me, there is no limit, no fixed form established for appearances; and someday God—or MY MIND—will recognize his own." Much more original and significant is the second of these works, a life of *Heliogabalus,* the false Antonin, who was cradled in sperm and buried in excrement. In him Artaud hails Anarchy's crowning achievement, i.e., "the full-length portrait of religious frenzy at its highest pitch, of aberration and conscious madness, the image of every human contradiction, and of contradiction in the very principle of things."

If we must consider these two works, in which Artaud

wallows in poison, as vacations from affliction rather than as creative achievements, the same cannot be said for *Le Voyage au Pays des Tarahumaras*. This magical text dominates everything he had written so far. It is the account of two episodes of his visit to Mexico in 1936, where he was doubtless attracted by the bloody legends of the Aztecs, the savage beauty of the country itself, the inhabitants' purity of countenance—and by peyotl. There can be no doubt that this journey among the Tarahumara Indians represented a kind of salvation for Artaud; never had his suffering, his inner agony corresponded so well to his vision of the world around him. The landscape he called "The Mountain of Signs" seemed to be the very reflection of his tortured self. The tangle of lines, the crevices in the rocks represented the accidents of his own substance and brought him nearer to that *petrifaction* he had hoped would put an end to his physiological and metaphysical anguish; at last he might become the equivalent of a natural phenomenon.

In the second part of this account, "The Peyotl Dance," we see him attending "the cataclysm which is his own body" among the ritual dances of the Indians who have grated the peyotl for him. The mind of Antonin Artaud rises above Antonin Artaud's body. And he undergoes every agony of the split personality, even to the point of craving purification by fire, death at the stake: "To this, I knew, my physical destiny was irremediably bound. I was ready for every agony of burning, and I awaited the first fruits of the flames, in view of a total combustion."

Here Antonin Artaud makes way for the person he calls familiarly enough, *Artaud-le-Momo* (in his native Marseille, "*le momo*" means "the madman"). And we pass, to borrow the terms already consecrated by the alchemists, from Artaud's "white period" to his "black period." To cross the threshold, to take the plunge, to change worlds—these paltry metaphors do not explain how Antonin Artaud, following Nerval and Baudelaire, Hölderlin and Nietzsche, found himself on the other side of the frontiers man must not cross, under penalty of no longer being recognized by his fellow-men.

It was during his return from a trip to Ireland that the terrible label *insane* was attached to his name, apparently as a result of the zeal of the medical officer and the captain of the ship on which he was forcibly taken at Dublin. The label remained for the nine years he spent in the asylums of Scotteville-lès-Rouen, Sainte-Anne, Ville-Evrard, Chezal-Benoit, and Rodez. He lost even his name as a poet: *Le Voyage au Pays des Tarahumaras* was published anonymously —no one knows why—in the August 1, 1937 number of *La Nouvelle Revue Française*. Two years had to pass before it was acknowledged, by publication of a letter from Artaud to Adrienne Monnier, that he was the author. The only word from him during almost the entirety of his confinement was *Les Nouvelles Révélations de l'Être,* published in 1937, also anonymously, by Éditions Denoël. It opens with this poem of the Double, of which I quote the beginning and the conclusion:

I say what I have seen and what I believe; and I shall attack whoever says I have not seen what I have seen.

For I am a relentless Brute, and it shall be ever thus until Time is no longer Time.

Neither Heaven nor Hell, if they exist, can avail against the brutality they have imposed upon me, perhaps so that I may serve them . . . Who knows?

In any case, so that I may be torn apart.

That which is, I can see with certitude. That which is not, I shall perform, if I must.

   . .    . .    . .    . .    . .    . .    . .    . .    . .    . .

It is a man in real Despair who speaks to you and who knows the happiness of being in the world only now that he has

abandoned this world, now that he is absolutely separated
from it.

Dead, the others are not separated. They still revolve around
their corpses.

I am not dead, but I am separated.

In the horoscope of the Tarot cards, in which Artaud
prophesies total Destruction—"but *Conscious* and *in Revolt*"
—what is striking is the fury of his expression, so characteristic of the entire "black period." This new mental world,
shot through with scorching or icy blasts, is a theater of
unknown rites. Yet we are carried through it by the wave of
mounting fury, and we dread its breaking upon us like the
downpour of a sacred tempest.

The *Lettres de Rodez* (1945), addressed to Henri Parisot
(who gave Artaud the great pleasure of seeing *Le Voyage au
Pays des Tarahumaras* published at last), take us into the real
life of Revelation. If we are unconcerned with the sorcery
and spells of which Artaud feels himself the victim and against
which he struggles so tragically, we are nevertheless affected
by the frenzied movement of his language, which attacks our
sensibilities with irresistible immediacy. Now that the thunder-
bolt has fallen, there is between Artaud and ourselves only
the dividing pane of the innocence we have lost, the experience we shall never have. We are shamed by the thought that
for so many years there should have been another kind of
"separation."

In 1946 Antonin Artaud resumed his place among us. His
friends celebrated the occasion: the homage paid at the
Théâtre Sarah-Bernhardt will not be forgotten. Among the
many notable persons who made a point of being there, I
shall mention only Charles Dullin, Colette Thomas, Roger
Blin, Jean Vilar, and Jean-Louis Barrault. Others were apparently "separated" from the man they were celebrating by

what is called success, sanity, literary (or simply Parisian) ambition—none of which could pass the test of purity constituted by the work Antonin Artaud had *lived*.

Between his release from the asylum at Rodez and that other "release" which he refused to call death, Artaud, at liberty, did a great deal of drawing and writing. He *knew* to within a few days when he was to leave us: the work he left us knew it too, perhaps. The fragments which have appeared here and there, in magazines or in books of a rather confidential aspect, permit our judgment little scope. It is an understatement to say that his *oeuvre* seems to us a major event: the extent of such a storm and the effectiveness of its destructions can only be measured with the passing of time.

To confine myself to what we can know of the immediate present, I shall list Antonin Artaud's last *manifestations*—which were also the last great joys of the man we loved and admired:

His contribution to the Lautréamont issue of *Cahiers du Sud,* in which he expresses, in the last section, the refusal of that breed of minds reaching from Poe to himself to serve as a "funnel for everyone else's ideas."

His lecture at the Vieux-Colombier, when he first recited "*Le Retour d'Artaud-le-Momo,*" "*Centre Mère et Patron Minet,*" "*La Culture Indienne,*" "*L'Insulte à l'Inconditionné*" —and then told the audience about himself in such a way as to inspire André Gide to write the following in the magazine *84:* "We had just seen a wretched man, a man excruciatingly tortured by a god, as if on the threshold of a deep cave, the sibyl's secret grotto in which nothing profane is tolerated, or as if, on some poetic Mount Carmel, a *vates* had been exposed, offered to the thunderbolts, to devouring vultures—a man both priest and victim. . . . One felt ashamed to resume one's place in a world where comfort consists of compromises."

His "encounter" with Van Gogh (during the great exhibition at the Orangerie) which he recorded in that little book full of the whirling suns that drove them both to despair: *Van Gogh le Suicidé de la Société*.

His exhibition, at the Galerie Pierre, of portraits which are not works of art, but which attempt to express "the ancient human history" imprisoned in the human face.

His recording for radio of *Pour en Finir avec le Jugement de Dieu*, with the assistance of Roger Blin, Maria Casarès, and Paule Thévenin.

And lastly, the publication of *Ci-Gît*, a poem as open as a grave, and of *Artaud-le-Momo*, which is not a poem but an immense "humbled cry" that "disgorges reality"—and serves, perhaps, as a prelude to a new state of health.

How much Artaud would have enjoyed seeing the first volume of his *oeuvres complètes* published! On the eve of his death, he was expecting the proofs of this substantial book, which he had sent to his publisher a year and a half before.

Besides *Suppôts et Supplications*, a three-hundred page compilation that may well comprise the principle work of his "black period," several supplementary chapters to the *Tarahumaras*, and a new essay on "The Theater of Cruelty," Artaud left an impressive amount of manuscript notebooks and a large number of letters, in which the features of Jacques Rivière's correspondent are further revealed and accentuated.

Those who were his friends will tell us what sort of man Antonin Artaud was. I had only approached him occasionally, yet the look in his eyes is still vivid to my own. And the "Nervalian" grace of his presence, rendering all the more poignant the tragic assurance of his powers of Revelation, remains with me like a secret effusion.

(1948)

*—Translated by Richard Howard*